GW01086356

For My Grandson David

Because of him these memoirs were written

And to My Other Grandchildren,

And Great Grandchildren

Hoping they will learn by each road they travel.

Also for My Children

Who suffered in silence listening to passages

from the book for their approval.

Thanking also my Aunt

(the one who platted her hair so fast),

for always being on the end of the phone,

and a friend who said he never got tired of listening to me.

Copyright © Lily Clark 2011

ISBN: 978 – 1 – 4477 – 9452 – 3

Lily Clark asserts the right to be identified as the author of this work in accordance with the Copyright Designs and Patents Act 1988.

This book is sold subject to the condition that it shall not, by way of trade or otherwise, be lent, resold, hired out, or otherwise circulated in any form without the consent of its author.

Published by Lulu

Printed in the United Kingdom

2 4 6 8 10 9 7 5 3 1

Cover Design and Graphics by Grace Durnford

Her you all Tom &
Denise, I hope you
enjoy my Journey.

Leroy Clark

INTRODUCTION

This is a story of a journey that has taken nearly a lifetime, and, when looking back, I ask myself: would I have traveled these roads had I of known where they would lead? But, everything is hindsight, and even now the roads on the map are still there, and still the decision of what road to take never changes; but this is part of my story, and you are invited to travel these roads with me, and as you take this journey you must think of your own, and maybe the next story I read will be yours.

Lily Clark August 2011

CONTENTS

Part 1.

A MAP UNFOLDS

I was born, so I was told, at 12 o'clock on a Saturday in 1938 in the East End of London. I always thought 'just in time for dinner' - still I do like Saturdays, I always have. I know you want to know my name, but what is in a name? It does not describe the person or tell you anything about them, does not tell you how they think or how they feel, or even how they will react to the things that are going to happen in their life.

Life, what a funny word, what does it mean? Perhaps, the ups and downs of experience, by which we hope we will survive. Why do I use the word "survive"? Is it because life is really a means of survival, a complex of roads on a map, and the decision to what happens to us is taken by which road we happen to choose, or a road by which we sometimes have no choice but to take.

I have taken many roads in my life and have stretched my mind as much as I can to see how far back down the first road my memory takes me, and still come up with going to a day nursery in Culmington Road, Ealing. I see a house big and double-fronted with lots of rooms and lots of stairs. I remember being given a spoonful of cod liver oil every day, and hating the taste, I would run out into the garden, and there I see myself spiting it out into the bird bath. Good job - birds can't tell tales, and I still hate cod liver oil.

Now I'm going to school and being introduced to the class. I can't remember if I enjoyed being in school at this time but, like all children, we have no choice but to go once we reach a certain age. I suppose our parents only hope that we will soon settle into the new routine, as we are always being told that the school years are the best times of our life. I remember there were long summer holidays, but there was no staying home as a war was declared between England and Germany in 1939, and because men were now being called to serve their country, women were now taking the place of these men and doing the jobs that had once been filled by them, and my mother was one of them. The year is 1943; I'm five years old, and the war is still raging - it's the time of Identity Cards, Ration Books, tins of powdered egg and food shortages.

The war has become very much part of my life even though I am still young and don't quite understand. At school we practice the drill of getting into lines and marching to the Air Raid shelter that is built in the playground. The teacher would blow a whistle pretending it's the siren which tells us that an air raid is about to start. We stand up quickly get into line and march.

But now I am not hearing a whistle, I hear a siren, and we are forming lines. We must remember the drill and get to the shelter as quickly as we can. The shelter is very narrow, and the walls rough and cold. There are lights, but they seem very dull. We stay there until the all-clear sounds, then it's back to our classrooms to carry on with our lessons as if nothing has happened. But there is no fear in my memory - I am not afraid - why do I not feel afraid?

That is how I remember the nights during the war: being taken from my bed and going to the air raid shelter that was dug deep in our garden. It always seemed to be so cold; we would put our coats over our pyjamas, Dad would carry blankets and Mum would carry me; later she would be carrying my sister and Dad would be carrying the blankets besides watching me. Out into the night air we would go as fast as we could to the bottom of the garden and to the Air Raid Shelter, our only place of safety.

Air Raid Shelters were also known as Anderson Shelters - they were put together with six corrugated iron sheets, bolted together at the top and with steel plates at either end, it measured 6ft 6ins. x 4ft 6ins (1.95m x 1.35m). The entrance was protected by a steel shield and an earthen blast wall. The earth that had been dug to make way for the shelter was now used to cover it. The only drawback was that it was not soundproof, so all the sounds of the raid could be heard, and sleeping was very difficult. Poor families who could not afford to buy one were given them free by the government, but if you earned more than £5 (pounds) per week you had to buy one yourself, and this would cost you £7.

For those people who did not have gardens and the protection of the Anderson Shelter, they would have a Morrison Shelter, which was kept in the house. It was made from heavy steel and could also be used as a table, it looked like a cage and people would shelter inside it during the raid. I try to imagine how it must have felt, knowing there was so much brick and mortar that could come down on top of you if the house had been bombed. There would be nowhere to run.

I can still remember the smell of the shelter; I don't know what it is, perhaps it's the damp. If the air raid went on for a while Dad would go back into the house to make tea and bring it down to us and, it's only now that I realise that he could have been in the wrong place at the wrong time. When the All Clear sounded telling us that the air raid was over we climbed out of the shelter, and when I looked up into the, sky it looked as if it was on fire, and the smell of smoke hung heavy in the air. I can still see in my mind the searchlights and the barrage balloons. The searchlights would light up the sky, hoping to catch an enemy plane in its vision, making it easer to shoot down, and barrage balloons, held with long steel wires acting as traps to snare the planes as they approached flying low. It all seems like a dream now. There were other families in our house, as there were four flats in all, but they never came down to the shelter; I never found out where they went, perhaps they had a Morrison .

I remember on one occasion we went to Horsindon Hill carrying lots of blankets with us, and we slept under the trees - I couldn't understand then why we did it but was told in later years that there

had been reports on the radio telling us that a bad air raid was expected and people were advised to get to a place of safety. Dad must have thought because this was not a built up area, we would be safe there. How I miss my Dad.

Now I have jumped ahead in my memory, as the next thing I remember is being on a train with Mum and my younger sister, it must have been my sister, but I only remember a baby. Dad is standing on the platform leaning on the door; I know we are going somewhere, but Mum is upset and she's crying. I know something is wrong, but what? I'm just excited about being on a train, but I don't understand why Dad is still on the platform. Again I find out years later that the government had advised that children should be evacuated away from the cities because of the bombing, so we went to South Wales, while other children went to the country, and some were even evacuated abroad.

"Evacuation" - this is a word that brings good and bad memories to so many people today. My sister and I were one of the lucky ones, as Mum came with us, but many of the parents were unable to go with their children, so they stood on the platforms watching the trains leave, waving goodbye to their children until the train was out of sight. They never knew what type of home their children would be going to, or what type of people they would be living with - what thoughts must have been going through their minds? The last thing they would see was their children with name tags pined to their coats, carrying gas masks in little boxes and their few possessions in bags or small cases and leaning out of the windows of the train waving until they could see Mum and Dad no more. Can you imagine what it must have been like during those days for both children and parents? This would be the first time that many of the children had ever been away from home, and very few would have ever been to the country. At first it must have seemed like an adventure, but after being away from their families for awhile, loneliness would set in and they would begin to miss home.

Now they would be living in strange houses or on farms with people they did not know and many of them were not made to feel welcome and were treated as an inconvenience. And as some families could only take one child, brothers and sisters were separated, which added to the problem of loneliness. Three point five million people, mainly children, experienced evacuation. When I have listened and read some of the stories from people who had to go through this time on their own, how glad I am that Mum came with us.

My Mum, how I wish you could have met her; she was tall with dark brown hair and big brown eyes. She loved clothes and big hats and always wore shoes with very high heels. I can see her now, standing in front of the mirror in the kitchen putting her lipstick on and when it was nearly all gone she would get a hair clip and dig out what was left in the bottom of the tube and then, with her finger, smooth it on her lips - funny the things we remember. I can see Dad, always so proud when he was with her or talking to people about her. She was the light in my Dads life.

She was much younger than Dad and married him when she was quite young. She had several jobs over the years to help with running the home. There were times when I would come home from school and wish she was there but I knew that this was not always possible, that is until later, when she managed to get work which could be done at home. She would make little bags for dolls, all different colours; she had a machine that you would put little eyelets on and then with her foot push down a pedal to seal each side of the bag and then add a little handle. I remember my sister and I would sit for ages folding the bags and then putting the eyelet on the machine for her, hoping to get them finished as soon as possible. They would be in bundles of one hundred and forty four. (one gross), and she would be paid by how many of these she could do.

I remember every day after school I would have to rush home and pick up a suitcase where the finished bags had been put, ready for me to take to the man who employed her. I would walk to the bus stop and get a 65 bus to Ealing Broadway, and then catch another bus to Hanwell. I can't remember the name of the road from which the man ran his business or the name of the man, but he would empty the case and then give me more to take back home to start all over again. Mum's sister was also employed by this man, but she worked in his house. How I hated having to do this journey every day and I did it for what seems such a long time. I hated getting on and off buses with a case that was heavy and I could hardly carry. How glad I was when Mum found another job; she was not there to welcome me home from school anymore, but at least I never had to make that journey ever again.

My memory of arriving in South Wales is not very clear; all I see is Mum knocking doors and hoping someone will take us in. I expect opening the street door to find a woman with two young children and being asked if we could stay could not have been easy for the people that lived there. Why did we leave home before we had a place to go? I find myself asking. Questions that now will never be answered. But someone must have felt sorry for us, as I see myself living on a farm, and I am happy.

I remember sliding down grassy banks, and going home with big holes in my knickers, of collecting blackberries and having one or two in the pot that had been given me to fill, and Mum saying "it will take more than that to make a pie," as I smile with dyed-blue lips, and the time I went running home asking for money to go to the sweet shop to buy ice cream; I don't know if I knew what it was, but by the time I reached home, it had melted, helped by my licking, with wafers stuck together, minus the ice cream. Mum said "where's the ice cream then?" I say "it melted Mum." She gives me one of her looks - I couldn't fool my Mum.

The only thing I remember about being at school in Wales is standing in a crowd by the school gate, of lorries going down the road and sweets being thrown over. I also see an old lady, maybe just old to me, pushing a bike and leaning it up against a wall; I don't know who she is or why she stands out in my mind, sad I never will. I wish I could remember more.

Even though the war was not over we returned home, home being an upstairs three-room flat, with a small scullery. Two of the rooms were at the front of the house, the other room looked out onto the back garden, and the scullery was a little room on its own at the side of the stairs that led to another flat at the top of the house. All the rooms opened on to a landing which meant there was little privacy, and as the people who lived upstairs would have to cross the landing, the doors to the rooms were always kept shut. My sister and I shared one of the rooms as a bedroom; Mum and Dad had the large room for theirs, which we called the front room, and then we lived in the smaller room which we called the kitchen. The scullery was really tiny; I often wonder now how we managed to wash and cook in such a small area and there was never any hot water unless we boiled a kettle until later, when Mum was able to buy a small water heater. Now we just turned a tap and hot water sprung forth - **this** we thought, was luxury. So much we take for granted now.

Our bathroom and toilet were on a lower landing, which we shared with the couple that lived in a flat along side this at the back of the house. After having a bath, I would run to the kitchen with a towel wrapt round me and then stand in front of the fire as the bathroom was so cold. When I was older, instead of having a bath at home I would go once a week to Ealing Baths. There I would buy a ticket at the kiosk and be given a number of a cubicle. Inside the cubical were a bath and a chair. I would fill the bath to the top and then rub the soap round and round in my hands to make bubbles in the water and then soak in luxury. Afterwards I would go back to the kiosk and buy a hot drink. Bovril was my favourite... I can smell it now.

Every Friday evening was the time when the flat would be thoroughly cleaned. Mum would sweep and wash the floors dust and polish until all was clean and shiny. We never had spray polish then, it came solid in a tin she would put it on the furniture and I would rub it off. All the time we were doing this Mum would sing. Her favourite songs were 'Molly Malone' not sure if this is the title but we only knew it as this, and 'Little Man You've Had A Busy Day;' how these songs must have gone down into my heart, as when I had my children, these were the songs I sang to them. There you are Mum - I have remembered some of things you taught me.

There are three things I remember about the bedroom I shared with my sister. First we shared a double bed; second I would wait for Mum to tuck me in and kiss me good night, and third I would wait a few minuets after she had closed the door and then get out of bed and go and sit on the window sill. The street lights were not electric as they are today, but gas and someone had to turn them on. We knew him as the Lamp Lighter. I would sit on the window sill and wait for him to turn on the street lights. He would come on his bike stop under each lamp, then with a long poll with a hook on the end pull down the chain that was attached to the lamp; this would bring the lamp to life. I never found out when he came back and turned the light off, as I was never awake when he did this. But the third part of this story has stayed with me all of my years. It was the times in winter when the snow fell, I would wait for Mum to tuck me in kiss me good night, then jump out of bed and find my seat on the window sill and watch the snow fall and because of the light across the road it lit up the flakes that fell. It was magical. But then Mum would suddenly burst in and tell me to get back into bed, saying it was time to sleep as I had school in the morning. But as soon as she left up I got again and was transferred back to this magical land. I am sure she knew that I would get out of bed when she closed the

8

door. Even now when the snow falls I look out of my bedroom window and turn towards the street light, and I am back once again to the childhood memory that brought me that magical joy and want those times all over again.

I don't see myself in the Air Raid Shelter at the bottom of the garden anymore, but in a very large under ground shelter that has been built across the road from where I live. Inside are rows of bunk beds with bare slats, but this time it is only a very brief picture. Almost as if I am looking at a photograph, but as I think about it I can feel the atmosphere, and there is that smell, and once again I am back in those dark days of World War Two.

As I wrote earlier there were four families in the house but only three of these would use the stairs, so every three weeks it was Mum's turn to sweep and wash them down. The lady in the downstairs flat just kept the passage clean. When I was older and had a bicycle I would keep it in the passage, but she was not happy about this and would complain to Mum. She would hear me come in then stand and watch to make sure I took my bike upstairs. Often I would hurt my legs catching them on the pedals as I struggled to carry it. But there was no change of heart from her - no feeling sorry for me.

Once a week Mum did the washing, but there was no washing machine. I can see her now with her arms in water up to her elbows; I remember how her hands were all red from using a scrubbing board. She would put the soap on the clothes first and then rub them up and down the board and as she did this you could hear the noise of the clothes being rubbed. Little did I know that I too would be doing the same thing in the future? Why do we say 'the good old days?'

In my bedroom there was a cupboard, and I can see hanging there our gas masks. We would carry these around with us, as there was

9

always a fear that during the air raid gas bombs would be dropped. I can't remember ever having to put mine on, but it was there just in case. For children under five they were issued with ones that looked like Mickey Mouse; you could get these in red or blue, so if the time came when they did have to wear it, they would not be so afraid. Hanging at the window in the kitchen was a thick blind, which was rolled down before we turned the light on each night. I am not sure what the blind was made of, but know it was black and we had to be very careful when we unrolled it as it would tear very easily. I can see now the little tears all along the sides. We would try not to let it drop too quickly or there would be another tear.

Air raid precautions now had to be taken and in society there are always those who want to do that bit extra, feeling the need to care. Men and women who give that sense of security when it is needed and in this case they were called A.R.P. (Air Raid Precaution) Wardens You would recognise them, as they wore helmets with a big W. on the front. They would walk the streets at night to make sure that no light was showing through the curtains, as the very smallest one could be seen by the enemy planes that flew overhead, and we did not want to help them in any way, banging on the door of your house if there was the slightest glimpse of a light. Now all the street lights were turned off so it was very hard to find your way around during the night. Often people would bump into each other. With darkness everywhere, it now became known as the Blackout. Streets became empty.

When the siren sounded Wardens would direct people to Shelters that had been built in the streets, as not all people were able to get home. Then they would unite family and friends if they had lost each other during the scramble to get to the shelters. They would sift through rubble after houses had been hit by a bombe or damaged by the blast – where did they find the courage to do this night after night I ask myself. If you check back in history we are told that two million houses, 60 per cent of these in London, were bombed; thirty two thousand civilians (people not in the forces) were killed and eighty seven thousand seriously injured

The bomb sites now became the playground for children and they would climb over the rubble and play at being solders. They would find pieces of the exploded bombs; this was called shrapnel and would be treated as treasure trove. But it was not always fun, as playing on these sites could be very dangerous. Not all bombs had exploded on impact and, once disturbed, came to life.

I remember how Mum and Dad never really got on with the couple that lived on the lower landing; they always seemed to be complaining about some thing. One of the times that stands out in my memory is when they pushed open our kitchen door and turned the light off. Here I need to tell you the reason why they did this. As I said earlier, there flat was on the lower landing, but instead of the electricity being separate we both used the same meter (I'm not sure how the electricity was paid for), so if they thought we had lights on too soon, they would complain. Mum had asked the landlord several times to get separate meters, but he always said he could not afford it, so this situation went on for years. For some reason, on this particular day, the light must have gone on early and as we were sitting having our tea, the door opened, this hand came in and switched off the light. When Dad realised what had happened, he turned and said to the hand, 'I will give you 10 seconds to turn the light back on' I cannot remember any other time when I felt that he was so angry. But before the 10 seconds were up, the light was back on.

Eventually they had a separate meter installed; Mum and Dad paid for this themselves.

The only other time I remember a bad confrontation with them was many years later. As I climbed the stairs, I could hear shouting coming from the landing, and there was this couple having an argument with my Dad. I don't think they expected to see me, as the wife, when she realised I was there, gave me a smile, as if she wanted my approval. She must have thought of me as still this little girl, but I was not the little girl any more - this time it was me who gave them the ultimatum, [I wonder where I learnt words like that]. They never bothered us again.

The road I lived in was long, with trees planted on the edge of the pavements, some of the houses had small front balconies, but I don't remember ever seeing anyone sitting on them; I'm not sure if they were big enough. The houses were very neat, with small front gardens, some of them had gates and short paths leading to the front door, but not all; one of them being mine.

I remember my front door being big and heavy, with four bells at the side; there were bay windows upstairs and down, with a small pointed window in the roof. At the side of the house was a wide ally big enough for cars to use. I remember also on the side of the house there was a wide crack that went from the top of the roof all the way to the ground, sometimes I would think about this and wonder whether the wall would fall down. But it never did as the house is still standing today (I hope they fixed the wall!).

To the left of the front door there was another door which opened into a narrow passage that was the length of the house; this led to the back garden. It was built into the house and was very dark as the only light that seemed to get in there was from a small window that came from the end door. It was here that coal was dropped into a cellar and it was here also that bins for the household waste was kept. There were three bins in all. One for rubbish, one for coal cinders and one for food waste, which was known as a "Pig Bin." Whether the food went to the pigs I am not sure. There was always the most awful smell that hit you when you opened the door, so you would never stay longer than was necessary. It was always open the door, lift the lid quick, empty your rubbish and run.

Writing this has reminded me of a funny story which I must tell you, though to me it was not funny at the time. I was older now, and on coming home from school, the first thing I did -like all children- I went to the food cupboard looking for something to eat. Mum was working and I could not wait for her to come home to give me my tea. But on opening the door of the food cupboard there was an awful smell. I started moving everything in the cupboard around trying to find what the smell was. At last I found the smell and on opening up the small package in my hand I looked and saw cheese which to me had gone mouldy. Thinking I was doing Mum a favour I went straight down the stairs and braved the pig bin That night Dad, when he was ready for his supper, went to the cupboard and was ages moving everything around and saying to Mum 'its not here'. It is there she says 'you're just not looking in the right place'. Still Dad is moving everything around getting more and more frustrated. What are you looking for? I ask him. My cheese he says. Oh that I say, I threw it away, it was mouldy. It was not mouldy he says that is what Gorgonzola cheese looks like. Go down to the bin and get it out he says. This was something I did not want to do. But down to the pig bin I go and dig my way through all the smelly food to find the cheese. Luckily it was still wrapped up. Dad enjoyed it anyway.

At the end of my road lived one of my friends, I can't remember when I first met her, she just always seemed to have been there. Sadly, her father committed suicide; I never found out why, then she moved away and I never saw her again; she did visit Mum some years later, and said she now lived in America, but sadly I was not there when she called. I wish she had left her address. I wonder where she is now, wonder what roads she took.

About five minuets away from my home, there were two parks, Walpole and Lamas; here I spent hours upon hours. Walpole had a small pond, where I would go to feed the ducks. Also I remember a cage where a lovely old parrot lived, her name was Lora - I can still see myself looking through the cage talking to her, trying to get her to say Hallo, and then all of a sudden she would answer, 'hallo'. Sometimes it seemed ages before I could get her to speak. I wonder who was having who on!

I especially loved going to the parks in the autumn and winter. In the autumn all the trees were golden, and then they would drop their leaves, and I would march through them kicking them high in the air as they crunched under my feet. In the winter, when the snow was thick, I would make snowballs; roll them till they were so big I could not push them any more. By the time I get home my feet and hands are so cold, I get close to the fire to get warm. Don't get too close Mum says you will get chilblains, but at that moment I don't care. Next day the cold is forgotten because off to the park I go and make snowballs all over again.

Lamas Park was different, it had no pond and no bird cage, but what it did have was SWINGS, how I loved these. Come rain or shine you could always find me, running from the roundabout, to the seesaw, back again to the roundabout, then sitting on a swing and pushing myself higher and higher. Why must our childhood end so soon?

But on the days I decided not too go to the park I would play in the road with my friend; there were very few cars then, not like today, so we would play with our skipping ropes seeing how long we could skip for without stopping, and when we got tired of that we played a game called Hop Scotch where numbers would be written on the pavement and a stone would be used to throw each time at a number. Then you would have to hop on one foot being careful not to put your other foot to the ground. How times have changed, how long since children played with skipping ropes and have they ever herd of Hop Scotch?

I remember another time when Dad made kites for us, with long tails

14

all made out of newspaper. I can see us now, running with them up and down the road, wishing the wind would catch them, and they would be lifted into the sky, but I am still running and see the kite crawling along the ground. We will try tomorrow Dad says may be there will be more wind tomorrow. But there was never enough wind.

Another one of my friends lived near Walpole Park, and I would sometimes go round to play with her after school; her house always seemed so big to me, and I always thought of them as very posh, as they seemed to be very well off. They had the entire house to live in, not just a flat; to me that was posh. I remember they had a Pekinese dog and when she had puppies I asked Mum if we could have one, but of course living in a flat and everyone out all-day, it was impossible, but I was still very disappointed. I remember one time when I went to play with her I noticed standing in the corner of one of her rooms was a box which had moving pictures in it. It was called television. I could not take my eyes of this - I had never seen anything like it in my life - to me it was magic, it had pride of place in the room and because the pictures were so small, in front of it stood a screen that was magnified to make the pictures look bigger. I remember the first time I saw it I ran home to Mum and told her about a box with moving pictures that had people that you could see and hear. She didn't believe me and thought I was making it up, so she gave me a clip round the ear. I wonder if she ever remembered doing that when later television became part of everyone's lives. I think I would remind her if she was here now (nasty).

As I turned into my road, there was a row of shops. I remember a bakers, a second-hand shop, and a sweet shop, with a grocer on the corner. Most mornings Mum would send me to get bread, we normally had a cottage loaf, and I would gently tear the top off and put my fingers inside and grab hold of the bread, which was soft and warm, into my mouth it would go, I would then push the top of the bread back, hoping Mum would not notice, it tasted oh so good, the

15

smell of fresh bread was just too much, and when Mum went to cut it, she would look at me, with that look in her eye, as each slice had a big hole in it (I wonder why she always sent me).

From the grocers, it was potatoes we bought most of all, as I think the shop was too expensive for us, so we would go further into town to get our main shopping. Alongside the shop was a big wall, there I would play with tennis balls, and sometimes slam them hard at the wall from the bat in my hand. Sadly it's no longer a grocer, but the wall is still there.

On Guy Fawkes Night, in the ally at the side of the house, we would have a big bonfire and lots of fireworks and because the grocer had sons, he was the one who always arranged it. I can see the fire now, and hear the jumping jacks and bangers, there not too loud, as I have my hands over my ears. The pretty ones I like best (I AM a girl!).

The sweetshop was my favourite (I wonder why?). The lady who owned the shop was very tall and very stern, and she never seemed to have any patience. I think I was a little scared of her so, although I loved her shop I was always glad when I had bought my sweets and I was back outside closing the door behind me. Her husband was shorter than her and stout; we never saw much of him, as he never seemed to serve us. But in 1954 when sweet rationing came to an end her shop began to be filled with so many sweets and chocolates the decision to choose became much harder.

Most Friday night's Dad would take us to the cinema; it was something we did for many years. Before we went he would give my sister and me money to go to the sweetshop. I would buy for him a half once of tobacco and cigarette papers. The papers would come in red or green packets, but he always wanted the red, I can't remember if I asked him why. Then we both had sixpence to spend on sweets, which would be about 2 ½ p today. How things have changed. What could you buy with 2 ½ p now? The sweetshop is not there any more, but my memory is.

One day as I was looking in the window of the second hand shop I saw a little cot and a small push chair for my dolly. I run home, can't wait to tell mum, now I am in the shop with her, but she said I could choose only one, what a decision, so I worked out in my young mind that at home I had an apple box, (lots of apples were packed in boxes in those days) which I had made into a cot, so I chose the pushchair. Now I can see myself walking along the street with my dolly in her new pushchair; I'm sure my dolly felt proud, I see myself so tiny. Is that really me? Next I see myself going to my Nan's and I am holding my dolly. She has a body made out of rags with a head of china, she has long silver hair but the hair is not real, but silver flaxen which Dad had sewn onto a piece of rag and then glued on to her head. I can see Dad now sitting at the table with the needle in his hand and I am watching him, I can't wait to have my dolly - hurry up Daddy. Now I have her in my hands and I'm combing her hair but it keeps breaking but I don't care to me she looks lovely - nobody has a dolly like mine. But now I'm on my way round to my Nan's and somehow now I have dropped her and the head has broken. I run all the way crying to my Nan. Can't remember what happened to my dolly and why she was not in her pushchair?

Whenever I had some thing new I would always go round to my Nan's (she was my mother's Mum). I would always want to share with her my good times and bad times; I loved my Nan; she was a big part of my life. She lived in Northfields, about twenty minuets away from where I lived; I would visit her with Mum and sometimes, even though I was still very young, would go to see her on my own. She lived in a nice house with two rooms and a scullery downstairs and three bedrooms and a bathroom upstairs. Even though there was a toilet in the bathroom there was also an outside toilet in the garden. I never liked using this one as I was always afraid there may be spiders in there and I hate spiders. Also I remember for toilet paper we used newspaper that was cut into squares and hung with string on a nail (Happy Days). The front room downstairs we called the Parlour and in it was a big black shiny piano which my uncle would play.

At the back of the house was a garden, and growing in it a large lilac bush that one day, thinking I was being kind, broke off several of the stems which had blossom on and took them into the house to give to Nan, but instead of a smile I was told to take them back outside as lilac was unlucky. It was only then that I began to learn how superstitious my Nan was. Overhanging the fence that divided the garden from the neighbours were branches from the neighbour's apple tree, but no one was allowed to pick the apples. That was totally forbidden.

I remember standing in her kitchen with two of my aunts who were just a couple of years older than me, we were all there getting measured for petticoats made out of Winceyette (a soft material). As we grew up together, I never thought of them as my aunts, they were more like sisters. I remember so many of the times we spent together it would be hard to write them all down but in my mind I always go back to standing in the kitchen watching them plaiting their hair and one of them was so fast at doing this I would look on in amazement, always wishing I had hair as long and as thick as theirs. But it was not to be.

My Granddad (my mothers Dad) - I only remember him as a small thin man, whether this is so I'm not sure, he always seemed to wear stripped shirts with a silver stud that was pushed into the top where a button should go. When he went out he would always wear a silk scarf which had long fringes each end; this he would put over his coat and with his cap on his head, be off to the pub. To me he was always down the pub.

I remember when he died the hearse stopped outside the pub, as a

18

mark of respect, never had seen that before. Wonder how much money he had spent in there over the years, or how much of that time he should have given to my Nan. As I think and remember, I feel sorry for my Nan.

She was a very big, chubby lady, and in those days it was common for people to have large families, and this was so of Nan. She had 14 children, but only 11 of them lived, then one died while serving in the Navy during the war. I remember her always wearing a piny which crossed over in the front and tied up round her back. She had long hair, which was always pinned close to her head, but it was never grey, always a lovely brown; she always looked the same to me and never changed in all the years I knew her. Sometimes when I went to see her she would ask me to go to the butchers at the top of the road, and there I would buy for her corned beef and breast of lamb, which the butcher would chop up for me. Then, with the lamb, she would make the most delicious stew in the entire world; mine never tasted like hers (or mum's).

Not far from the butcher's there was a tap dancing school, where I would go once a week for an hour, for which I would pay sixpence (2 ½ p.). I remember standing in a line with lots of other girls learning to 'shuffle hop step'. I know I can still do that. 'No effort,' didn't keep it up though.

On one of my visits to Nan's house I heard a funny noise coming from the garden and, looking through the glass doors that led into the garden, there was a big white duck running around. I couldn't take my eyes off it, there it was, quite happily making noises and pecking at the ground. I found out later it was a goose, 'still a duck to me.' When I went back a few days later, there was my Nan with the goose across her lap being plucked. 'Poor Goose' I wonder where Granddad got it from, maybe the pub.

Just before Granddad died, I remember him being in hospital. I went to see him with Mum and while we were there one of my other aunts turned up to see him, and she was all in black, even had large black earrings on, and when Granddad saw her, from his bed he said "I ain't dead yet!" Funny really, because that is the last thing I remember about him, and the last thing I remember him saying. No wait a minute, I have just remembered one more thing. He would take off his wide belt that held up his trousers and hang the buckle on a nail and then sharpen his razor on the belt, going backwards and forwards at such speed. How could I have forgotten that? Goodbye Granddad.

I don't know how Nan felt when granddad died, as she never spoke to me about it. I suppose its like all grownups, we try to protect the young from our grief, I wonder some times if that is the right thing to do.

I see Nan still, sitting in her kitchen, putting a spoonful of Epsom salts in a saucer, and then she would pour some of her tea on to the salts, stirring it before drinking. Every day she would do this; she never said why, but she did live to be 80, so it must have done her some good.

I still remember the Christmases when we would go to Nan's, it would be either Christmas day or Boxing Day; I always hoped that my cousins would turn up as well. This was the one time we would be allowed to go into the parlour (we would never go in there normally). We would stand around the piano and my uncle would play, and we would all join in the different songs, trying to remember the words. Before we went I would really nag Mum and Dad to go as I enjoyed these times so much. I remember we would have to walk, as there were no late busses then. When I look back, the night always seemed to be crisp, being winter, and I would look up at the stars, and as I walked with Mum and Dad, I felt really happy: oh what a good memory. I look up where I am now, and you can't see the stars clearly any more, too many street lights. How I wish sometimes we could turn back time. Or turn off the lights.

Another time that stands out to me is when we are walking along the road and there on the pavement is this little black kitten, who is crying. We pick it up, and want to take it home; Mum and Dad looked around, but there are no houses to see where it might of strayed from, so they gave in, and guess what, we called him Blackie. We had him for 16 years - we loved that cat! I remember sometimes as I walked to school he would follow me to the end of the road, and when I came home after school, there he was sitting on the wall as if he had been waiting for me. He loved cheese so we would put a piece on the edge of the table and he would pick it up with his paw, then put it in to his mouth, we never got tired of watching him do this. One time he was really ill, so we took him to the vet, and he had to have an operation; he was so poorly, we wondered if he would live, but he did. I remember how I screamed one night when I walked into the scullery and there was a mouse, Blackie came to my rescue. 'Good old Blackie'.

There was no television in every home like there are today; there were no computers, no CD players, and no videos. For the grown ups there was radio, but for the children there was 'Saturday Morning Pictures' oh what you have missed! This was the highlight of the week for me and hundreds of children everywhere. We would queue with our money in our hand waiting for the ticket that would take us on adventures all over the world. We would fly to the moon, visit cities beneath the sea, fight lions in jungles and bears in forests. We would ride horses and swim with sea monsters. Then shout at the goodies and boo at the baddies. We would stamp our feet, clap our hands and sing with the loudest voices. There was nothing like Saturday morning pictures.

Lots of Sunday mornings Dad would get me up early; we would get the train to the East End of London and go to 'Petticoat Lane' Market, a market that has been around since the seventeen hundreds.

What an adventure that was for me, I loved it, all the stalls and the people. Dad buying me hot chestnuts trying to take off the peel, but too hot to hold in my hand, cant wait to put them in my mouth (bring back hot chestnuts!). I've not been there for years; I don't expect it's the same, but maybe the man with the chestnuts is still there.

I remember one time, when we went to the market; Dad bought me two white mice and a little cage with a wheel inside, and one morning the people in the downstairs flat rang our bell, and asked us if we had lost our mice as there were two running up her bedroom curtains. Can't remember what happened to the mice after that, somehow they disappeared. Another time we found a pigeon in the street that had hurt itself; we put it in a little cage and nursed it till it was better and we called it Paul. Why Paul? Maybe because Mum used to say a little rime to us 'Two little dickybirds sitting on a wall, one named Peter one named Paul, fly away Peter fly away Paul; come back Peter come back Paul. She would put a piece of paper on a finger of each hand (the paper pretending to be the birds) then throw a hand over each shoulder, then she would bring her hand back, the bird had gone. Then, she would throw her hand back over her shoulder again, and when she brought them back there they were, I never knew were the birds had gone, or how they came back. My Mum was very clever.

Because Mum came from a big family I had lots of aunts and uncles, some I saw more than others, which also meant lots of cousins. One of her younger sisters would come round quite often and I remember how she would sit on our bed and read us stories. She was very close to Mum and Dad, and because Mum was much older, took her under her wing; the sad thing about this is once she married she never really cared any more about Mum. I wonder how Mum felt. Poor Mum. Sad how we so easily forget.

I had one cousin I was really close to, who lived at Finsbury Park. I would get the train from South Ealing station to her house, it would take me over an hour to get there; I can't believe I made this journey on my own as I was still quite young. How times have changed. I remember going to Môn sell Park with her and playing on the swings. There was one we called the Maypole, it had ropes which hung from the top of the poll, and we would loop the rope around our arm and then run and jump and we would fly through the air; I don't think I could do that now, mind, would be good to try.

Coming home from the park we would often meet the crowd from the football ground (Arsenal, I think); there were hundreds of men, but we were never afraid. Sometimes if we had any money we would stop at a little sweetshop and buy chocolate powder or lemonade powder; I would lick the end of my finger and put it in the little bag then into my mouth would go my finger and it was heaven, I can't remember what flavour I liked best. But I know I stood for ages trying to decide which one to choose, this shopkeeper must have had lots of patience. Where have all the little sweetshops gone?

Some evenings when I was with my aunt and uncle, they would take us to the pub. They would go in, and we would wait outside, then they would bring out crisps and lemonade. At this time children were not allowed in pubs, but they would never leave us alone at home, so we went with them - don't feel sorry for me having to wait outside, I loved going with them, to me it was a special time..

When it was tea time we would lay the table, each of us having a plate and at the side of the plate was put a pin, then on to the plate would go a handful of winkles (shellfish). I have never known anybody get winkles out of the shell as fast as my uncle. With the pin you would take off what we called the eye, and then dig out the winkle. But with pepper and vinegar and bread and butter they were lovely - can you still buy winkles today?

Sometimes my uncle would go out on his own, and then come in late at night, and I would be in bed with my aunt and cousin, we would hear him come in and know that he was merry. I remember him calling my aunt's name, and she saying "shhh""pretend we are asleep". I'm sure he must have had a bad head in the morning

When it was time for me to go home my aunt would walk me to the station, she would wait for the train and then put me in the carriage with the guard, and ask him to keep an eye on me and make sure I got off at the right place. I still had a bus to get, but always got home safe.

Sadly my aunt and uncle are no longer here, but I am sure they would be happy to know that I still remember all the good times they gave me, and how much they must have cared for me, and how they had an influence in my life.

One day there was a ring at the door and on the doorstep was another one of my aunts - she was married to one of Mum's brothers. I remember that she was crying. Next there was another ring at the door, and when Dad went to open it, there was my uncle looking for my aunt. Meanwhile, Mum had pushed her under the table in the kitchen. It was a big square table and on it was a thick cloth covering it. The cloth had a long fringe all the way round which nearly touched the floor, so he was not able to see her. I never found out why she was crying and why Mum pushed her under the table. I wish I had asked Mum when I had been old enough to understand.

Most Sundays I would go to my Nan's. If the girls were not there they would be at Sunday school, so off I would go to meet them. I can still see myself standing around wishing the sermon would hurry up and finish. I couldn't wait for them to come out, there was always one more hymn to sing - why are some hymns so long? Or so it seemed to me. From there we would go to the park which was just a few yards away and there again we would play on the swings - what innocent fun. I remember one time we were on a roundabout and we were pushing it around so fast it banged against the poll in the middle, and a finger got in the way, we ended up in the casualty department. Not my finger, I'm glad to say. Cruel.

I don't remember the time the war finished; I only remember there was a party in the street, and every one was happy. A long table was put in the middle of the road, with chairs on both sides. All the children from my road and the roads around were there; shame I can't remember what we had to eat, but whatever it was, all the Mums and Dads must have done their best, as food was still very hard to get at this time. When we finished eating, all the chairs and tables were cleared away and games were now played. I see myself running in the sack race; I can't remember if I won, and now I have a spoon in my hand for the egg and spoon race, but it can't be an egg on the spoon as these are still rationed so what can it be? I still don't know if I won.

As a child, shopping with Mum was always some thing special, and one day, walking to the shops at South Ealing, we went into the greengrocer's and, looking up I saw hanging from the ceiling, a big picture and asking 'what are they Mum?' Bananas, she said. Even though she tried to explain what they were, I did not understand. I can't remember the first time I tried one. Now we can buy them everyday.

When you see all the food in the shops today it's very hard to imagine a time when food was so scarce, a time when you would queue for hours and by the time you got to the counter they would say 'it's all gone.' A time when mums would have to go back home and tell their family 'there's not much to eat today.'

During the war years and for a time after, food and clothes were difficult to get, and to make sure that everyone had their share; the government rationed food and clothes. I will give you a small list of what each adult was allowed; remember these amounts would have to last them for one week.

Butter   2 ounces =   50g.
Bacon   4 ounce =   100g.
Sugar   8 ounces =   225g.
Cheese   2 ounces =   50g.
Milk   3 pints   =   1800 ml
1 egg per week.

Meat to the value of 1shilling and tuppence per week; that would be about 6 pence today0

Sweets were rationed in 1942. Each person was allowed half a pound [200 grams] every four weeks.

Even soap was rationed in 1942. Rationing altogether lasted fourteen years from 1940 until 1954.

As you ponder over these amounts and they are only a part of all the items that were rationed. I hope it will give you an idea of how families had to cope with not only the bombings and evacuations and the loss of loved ones at home and those in the armed forces, but how they would have to try and feed there families; parents often going without so there children could remain healthy. Remember that at this time there was no National Health, so a visit to the doctor had to be paid for.

Here there is one story I must tell you about, in case I forget. On our way to the station on a day out with the family, we looked into a greengrocer, and they were selling raffle tickets, the prize was two lemons (can you imagine that now?). Dad went in and bought one raffle ticket. I can't remember if we spoke about it again, but guess what: he won! I know Mum never knew, as Dad tied them together with a bit of string and hung them over the door of our kitchen so she would not notice them when she walked in. He said for us not to look up and give the game away, when she finally came home she looked at our faces and knew we were up to something. She had a look which said 'ok what's going on' and soon my sister and I were looking at the ceiling. I will never forget the joy that was in that house that day (tears in my eyes).

When I look back and remember my Dad, I always think of the times we spent together, there was nothing too much or nothing that could not be put right by my Dad. He watched over us all with the love and care of someone who treasured what he had.

Now I must tell you something about my Dad. He was born in the East End of London and was one of a large family. As far as I know, he had four sisters and two brothers. Occasionally we would travel on the train to see them, we would visit one, and then make the rounds to the others, I don't remember being close to them, but one time does stand out in my mind. We had travelled by train to the East End to visit one of my aunts, and crowds were standing on the pavement. When Dad asked my aunt about this she told us that the King and Queen were visiting the area, so I asked if I could run to the top of the road to see them. When I got there the people were waving flags and shouting. I pushed my way to the front of the crowd, then I saw this big black car and as it passed I saw the King and Queen and the two princesses through the windows. I don't know if I really knew who they were, but it must have had some impression on me, as I still remember after all these years.

When I asked Dad about his life, he never really said much. What I do know is that he had a twin sister who had died as a baby, and then his Mother died when he was still a young boy. So he was sent to an orphanage where he stayed until he was old enough to become a house servant. Later he joined the army, serving in India for many years. He always said that after having such a sad childhood, joining the army was the best thing that had happened for him.

27

When he finally left the forces he went back to the East End, but of course had no home to go to, so he went to his sisters, but not one of them would take him in, so he found the Salvation Army and they gave him food and a bed till he found a place to live. He always said he was grateful to them and never forgot what they had done for him.

It makes me wonder why he bothered with his family, but there we are - that was my Dad. He did say that eventually he was able to get a flat but lost it when it was hit buy a bomb. He managed to find another one, which he always spoke about with such pride. Then he met Mum, married her and then they had me. Sadly this flat also was hit by a bomb, so Dad decided it was time to move away from the East End of London and that was how we came to live in Ealing.

He hardly ever spoke about his father; I have a feeling that they never got on. Only once I remember seeing him, and that was when we went to visit him in hospital; he just seemed like a very old man with his head resting on a pillow. (I wish I could find out more about him.)

I know that one of Dad's sisters was married to a man that was a maintenance inspector with the London trams. I remember visiting him many years later with Mum and Dad, but he was not with my aunt any more, there was another women with him who he called his 'Housekeeper'.
I remember four cousins I had from this side of the family, but did not spend any time with them, maybe if we had lived closer it could have been different. To be fair, I have not even thought about them till writing all this down.

So many things happen in our lives; how can we remember everything, I ask myself. Why do some events stand out more than others, such as the time Dad and I went to buy coke from the Gas Works at Kew. This will seem very strange today, as I can't

28

remember a time when any of my grandchildren ever lived in a house with open fires, but I must tell you the story (coke by the way, is coal but with all the gas taken out).

Coal years ago was very hard to get even after the war, and most homes were kept warm by this means, there were fireplaces in nearly all of the rooms in the houses at that time. The fire was lovely to sit by and keep warm, and many a time I would watch the flames, and see them dancing, each one telling their own story, and in the winter we would buy chestnuts, split them, then put them on a shovel, and then lay the shovel on top of the coals until they were roasted. We would all sit waiting for the first one to be ready, never sure who would be the first to taste heaven.

There were only two draw backs I can remember about open fires. First, if we moved away from the fire, we very soon felt the cold - so nobody ever wanted to move. Second, we had to clean out the grate of ashes before we could relight it. I remember saving the cinders if they were big enough so we could use them again, nothing was ever thrown away if it could be reused.

I can't remember why we went to the Gas Works to get the coke; I assume it must have been hard to come by. As coal was rationed during the war, many of the miners had to join the armed forces, so there were far fewer working the mines. Dad said 'pretend you are on your own.' So I stood and waited with a sack in my hand. They filled the sack and then put it on the pushchair I had with me. It was not money I gave them - I seem to remember a ticket. Dad told me that when I had got the coke to wait outside the gas works, next minute, he turned up with another sack full, so that day we had two sacks of coke (I have a feeling it should have been just one sack per family). But we couldn't get on a bus this time, so we had to push the pushchair all the way home, which must have taken us ages; not only was it a long way, but it was very hard to push.

Years later when I told this story to my children they said 'We never knew we had a coke pusher for a mother.'

During the war Dad worked for Woolwich Arsenal where they made the armaments. He travelled around the country inspecting factories that had been taken over for this purpose. Many stories he told me about this time, but the one that stands out the most is when he had to go to the north of England. He was going to be away for a few days, so he decided to take Mum and me with him (my sister had not yet been born). He had taken us to the cinema in the evening and while we were watching the film it was announced that an air raid was about to start. Dad wanted to leave the cinema, as he felt unsafe in there, but Mum did not want to go. But soon Dad became very agitated and in the end just grabbed her and with me under his arm marched us outside. He said that they had not gone very far before there was a direct hit by a bomb on the cinema. He pushed Mum and me into the gutter and just lay on top of us till it was safe to move. He said when they looked back everything had gone, and there was just fire.

When I see old newsreels of that time and see the blitz as it was, I ask myself how people could possibly have survived. Then I remember I was there and survived because of my Dad.

Here I must tell you another story. Mum and Dad decided that they were going to buy Dad a new overcoat, so they counted up all the clothing coupons they had, and then went to West Ealing. We spent ages going around all the shops, but could not find the coat he wanted. So in the end we came home not with an overcoat, but curtains for the front room. The sad thing about this is that when Mum hung them up, they were so light in colour and with the sun on them you could not see the pattern and they looked just like sheets up at the window. She never liked them and was always sorry that she had bought them. But this was a story we told and laughed at for many years, so perhaps it was not a disaster after all.

So here once again the matter of coupons plays a big part in people's lives just as food was rationed so too were clothes. Today there are so many clothing shops to choose from that buying clothes seem more of a chore than a pleasure.

There was a saying then of 'Make Do and Mend' - this was a slogan that was given to us by the government. But you had to make do and mend on 48 coupons a year. So what might you get for this? Again here is a short list of some of the items for children.

Cardigan 5 coupons.
Trousers 6 coupons
Skirt   4 coupons
Shoes   2 coupons
Socks   1 coupon
Dress   5 coupons

So next time you buy yourself that special dress or that trendy pair or trousers, imagine counting your coupons and then think of the disappointment you would have if you did not have enough.

Certain days also stand out in my memory, like the time we went to South End on Sea. It was November 19th 1947. Why do I remember that day so clearly? It's because it was the day before Princess Elizabeth, as she was then named, got married. Dad had bought a tandem and later fitted an engine on to the front wheel. We would start the engine by pedalling as fast as we could; I can still see us now, being half way down the road before it would burst into life. It never seemed to start straight away. I have a feeling that all the neighbours were watching us from their windows - I can see all the curtains twitching, eyes peeping through, either trying to start the engine with us, or having a good laugh. I expect we made their day.

Mum and my sister went on the train to South End, but Dad and I went on the tandem. I ask myself, why did we not all go by train? I cannot think of any other reason than he was really excited about the tandem having an engine and he wanted to try it out. .I can't remember who got to South End first. The only other thing I do remember about that day is that on the way home it poured with rain, so we stopped in a small café and drank hot tea, and I was made a fuss of by the people in there, as I was so wet. Because of the wedding the next day most of the roads in the city had been blocked off. Good-job-Dad knew his way around London, as we got home safe. That's all I remember about that day.

I don't think Dad had the tandem for very long, for soon he was riding a motor bike. He had several of these over the next few years; the one that stands out in my memory is a Matchless. All the motor bikes would have a sidecar in which, Mum and my sister would sit, and I would ride pillion with Dad with my arms round him holding on tight. I can still hear him trying to kick start the bike in the mornings when he was rushing to get to work and the silly thing would not start. He would end up coming back upstairs, waiting for a while and then trying again. Are the curtains still twitching?

One of the things my Dad loved most was music. He said that when he was in the army, he had played the drums in a small band. He was always tapping two forks on the cups and saucers, plates and sauce bottles as we were eating our food at the table. We would love to watch him do this. The wireless (this is the old fashioned word for radio) would play the music, and then into his hand would go the forks - I'm sure he imagined he was back in his younger days. We try to copy him, but we never get it right. He was also a collector of records and he loved to dance to the music of Victor Sylvester (who's that I hear you say?). I can see him now dancing with Mum, and then when it was my turn I would put my feet on top of his and he would glide me around the room. Oh why can't I have those days back again?

I remember one time we went to Petticoat Lane and while we were there Dad bought a record that he had long wanted. We carried it all the way home, first by train and then by bus, so careful not to break it. When we got home it was put on a chair, and guess what: I sat on it!!

The records we would play on a record player that stood in the corner of the front room, it was tall and narrow and stood on four legs. Before we could play the records we would have to wind it up with a handle that came out of the side, then we would have to swing what we called an arm over and forward and then place the tiny needle that was screwed in to the end of the arm onto the record very gently. Because the needles did not last very long, we always had to buy new ones. I would go to Squires, the piano shop at Ealing Broadway. I remember it being a very posh shop, or so it seemed to me, and there I would buy a little tin that was filled with these little needles.

Later Dad bought the most beautiful radio gram; we did not have to buy needles any more, as it was electric. This became his pride and joy.

Even though it must have been hard for Mum and Dad, we at no time then seemed to go without the necessities of life. There was always food on the table, and we always looked clean and tidy. I remember they bought my sister and me coats which were both the same, they were bright red, with wing like frills on the shoulders and had black piping sewn onto them. I hated it, firstly because of the wings, and secondly, I hated being dressed the same as my sister. We always seemed to be dressed the same. Now I can see a tartan skirt with a white frilly blouse, with a waistcoat on top; I don't seem to mind this, but I still look like my sister. I always said that if I had two girls I would never dress them the same.

For some reason my socks come to mind - they would always slide under my heel, and I was forever pulling them up, then the tops would stretch, and that would make them worse. Sometimes Mum would make garters to go round the top of the sock, hoping this would keep them from sliding down, but they never worked. Why have I suddenly remembered my socks?

Due to all the coal that was burnt to keep people warm in those days, and also the factories and trains that continually used this as well, London was known for its fog, which also turned into smog, this contained all the bad fumes from the coal. Thousands of people would die each year from the harmful effects of this. I remember sometimes the fog would be so thick that you could not see you're outstretched hand in front of you. Often you would see the buses creeping along the road, the conductor instead of being on the bus, would be out in front with a torch in his hand, trying to guide the driver. These became known as 'Pea Soupers.' Perhaps there's something to be said for radiators after all.

I remember one Saturday night, we had been to the pictures, and when we came out, the fog had come down and we could hardly see our way home. Dad put my sister on his shoulders and I held Mum's hand; we were so glad when we finally found our front door ('there's no place like home').

The years have passed now and I see myself in the junior school, I don't have a lot of memories of this time, I know it was a mixed school of boys and girls, but I never seem to want to be there. All my school life I could not wait for the bell to ring to tell me it was home time. I hated going in the mornings and couldn't wait to leave at the end of the school day. I have never found out why I felt like this. I wish I knew. On the day I finally left school altogether, the other girls were crying, but not me. I think that day was one of the best days of my life.

One of the teachers who stand out in my memory was a great big woman who was such a bully. On a Monday when we had to take our dinner money in, I would either be late and remember it, or be early and forget it, I don't know why. Then one day she got really angry with me and pulled me out in front of the class and slapped the back of my legs with a ruler and I really cried. I felt terrible crying in front of the class, and I remember thinking afterwards, nobody in school will make me cry again, and they never did, (not that I was an angel). I can still see her walking up and down the rows of desks with that ruler in her hand, and she always seemed to be shouting. Sad, that I only remember her for this.

Not far from my school was a greengrocers on one side of the road and a sweetshop on the other side. Some mornings Mum would give me a penny and on the way to school I would stop at the greengrocers and ask for a Pen'ath of Specs; this was fruit that had not been sold the day before or was bruised. These were always kept in a wooden box on the floor. If the greengrocer never had any, I would cross the road and go into the sweetshop and choose a few sweets that were on a small table at the side of the counter. I couldn't get many as I only had a penny.

Now I am older, and I see myself in the senior school, this time it's all girls. Things don't seemed to have changed too much - I still do not like being here, but now I have become the games captain, as I have found that I am very good at sports, and running seems to be the thing I do best. I run for the school on sports day, I come in first and have a medal in my hand. I love Netball and Rounders - I see myself going to other schools to play in matches and having tea and sandwiches after; those were the best times. I think maybe I could still play Rounders, but netball and run I don't think so

As I have told you I never liked school and on one occasion I played truant and decided to go to the pictures in the afternoon instead. Unfortunately I got found out. The following morning I was stood in front of the whole school at assembly time; there the head mistress told the school that I had done this because I did not want to do my poetry exam. How wrong she was. I did it because I did not want to be there. I was told that I had to go and stand outside her room after I had finished my dinner each day, till she decided when it was enough. I went once.

There was one privilege that you were given in your last year and that was being allowed out of school after we had eaten our dinner, so I would go with some of the other girls over to Lamas Park which was not too far from the school, and there we would meet up with the boys from the local Boys-only Grammar school. They wore caps as part of their school uniform and these the girls would grab, and then throw them to each other, hoping to get chased and then caught. Why, as I write this do I giggle, maybe because I can see it all in my mind, and want to bring back those innocent days of childhood.

There is only one girl I seem to remember from senior school. I would go round to her house quite often. I remember her mother showing me how to back comb my hair to make it look much thicker and then try a new style. She was always talking about clothes and telling me all about the things she did as a teenager.

Some evenings I would rush to my friend's house, then I would back-comb my hair, put makeup on (borrowed from my friend's mum), trying to make myself look older. Then my friend and I would go to the local dance hall. Her mum would give us the money for the entrance fee. Sometimes they would let us in, other times we were told we were too young. I loved to dance. The thought of dancing to a big band was just too much and when we were turned away I was always so disappointed. I never told my parents and they never found out.

As a teenager I began to take more interest in the clothes I wore, but clothes were expensive to buy and I could not always have new ones, so I would go to a house that was used as a place to swap second hand clothes; this was run by the W.V.S. (Women's

Voluntary Service). This is how it worked: You would take the clothes that you no longer wanted to them, and then they would give points for each item according to the type of clothing and the condition it was in. Then they would add the points up, now you could choose clothes from the racks which were full of items that other people had brought in.

I would go through the racks looking for something I liked and checking the number of points that was pinned to the item on a little piece of paper; then I would add up the amount of points against the points I had. I was sad sometimes because I would see something I really liked but did not have enough points.

When I read back on the first part of my life it all seems very gentle, and I suppose it was, I was one of the lucky ones. I had good parents who loved me, who did the best they could, considering the times that we were living in.

Many of the things I remember are not always in the right order as it was such a long time ago, but it will give you some idea of the life I had as a young child to when I left school. Till now all decisions were made by my parents, now things begin to change - as a teenager leaving school I start to take a different road, now I begin to make decisions of my own.

Part 2.

A NEW ROAD

Just before I left school, I went twice a week for one hour to an evening class to learn shorthand and typing, for which Mum paid 2 shillings per hour [10p]. The typing I seemed to manage, but never did succeed with the shorthand. Mum always wanted me to go into office work, because that was thought of as a much better job than working in a factory or a shop. I was given no choice about this. I had to do what my parents thought was best for me. I did argue with them about it, but to no avail. For some reason I always wanted to work in a Chemist shop; don't know why.

Now I am nearly fifteen and leaving school is just around the corner; I am counting the days, can't wait to leave. The school gave me an employer to contact, and though I can't remember if I was given more than one, I started work as soon as I left school, as there was no shortage of jobs then. I would get a train to Hammersmith Broadway and then walk for about 10mins to my place of employment, which was at Lyons Cadby Hall. This is a very old company and was started in the 1800's, and it was at this factory that all manner of foodstuffs were made such, as individual pies, Swiss Rolls, all types of bakery, and so much more. A lot of the buildings were pulled down in 1983 and rebuilt in 1990, and I am sure this once again 'they' say is progress, but my memory is back there and the part the old buildings played in my life.

I started in the post room, not sure if this is what it was called, as once again my memory lets me down, but I do know I was known as a messenger girl, or a junior. All the internal and external mail would come to this small room to be sorted, and I would then take the bundles of mail round to the different departments.

Sometimes I would have to take letters or parcels to different people and places in the city and I would travel on buses and trains to deliver these. I learnt to find my way around all the little back streets; it was a new adventure - I went to places I never new existed - to hotels that seemed so big - I could not believe that people lived in such luxury; and shops that seemed just like fairy land. As I remember now, I feel the thrill of it all and see my eyes big like saucers.

Because my place of employment was so big I had large bundles of mail to carry, so I would take the lift to the different floors. The one person that stands out to me at this time is the man who operated the lift; he was lovely, always smiling and never cross, even though sometimes he would have to wait either for people running to get the lift or me dropping the mail. He wore a white jacket with a flower in his lapel. With his finger on the button he would say 'You OK there' in a singing Welsh accent.

While working here I met a boy a little older than me, and each night we would walk to the station together and before I caught my train home, we would stand and talk; I wish I could remember what we spoke about, I know I was flattered; I never spent any other time with him and soon forgot about him when I finally gave this job up. I was paid once a week on a Friday - the grand some of £2.pounds, 9. shillings and 11 pence. (This would be about £5 pounds today.) I would give Mum £2 pounds and out of that she would give me my train fare every day; also I would get a clothing check for 10.pounds every five months from a clothing company. I would pay back 10 shillings a week. Then start all over again. The 9 shillings and 11 pence I kept for myself.

I was never allowed to wear any makeup before I left school (with Mum's knowledge), so my first big adventure was to buy lipstick, foundation cream and an eyebrow pencil. I was always going to the cinema and would see the film stars and wanted to look just like them. Each Friday I would collect my wages, which were given to me in a little brown envelope. I had never had so much money. Now I really was grown up.

On the way home each payday I would stop and buy Mum a small bunch of violets from an old lady that had a stall at the entrance of the train station. It had to be violets, as I had so little money to spend, as my 9 shillings and 11 pence had to last me the week, and they were the cheapest flowers she had. Even now, all these years later, every time I see violets it reminds me of the smile I would get from Mum. (I wonder if she even liked violets; I never thought to ask.)

I was happy at that time and looked forward to going to work each day, but I only stayed in the post room for about a year and then they moved me to another department. So now I see myself in a much bigger office and seem to be in a corner all on my own. I am not happy and no longer look forward to work each day and soon decided to leave, so the next place I see myself working is The Firestone Tyre Company on the Great West Road. One of the outstanding features about this factory was its building. It was designed in Art Deco, and if you stood and looked at it from the front it was magnificent. It was built in 1928, but demolished in 1980, and all that reminds us now of the building that once stood there are the gates, which they decided to leave, along with a few lamps. Once again I am working in an office. This time the office is on the factory floor. Now they say that we all have embarrassing moments in our life, so here is one of mine while I was working for this company.

The office was just an annex that had been built on the factory floor; it was not very big and had a dividing wall which made it into two smaller offices. In the first office the manager would have his desk, and in the office I was in, there were two desks - one for me and one for the other girl I worked with. On each of our desks we had a typewriter. The chair I had was one which you would swivel on an axel to either make it go up or go down. The only thing was my chair used to rock as well as swivel. One morning the manager had a meeting in his office with three of the supervisors off the factory floor. Because the dividing wall was made up of a glass partition you could see into each office. I had been to the filing cabinet and now I wanted to sit down, and guess what? – The minute I sat down on my chair it swivelled and rocked at the same time. There was I looking like a trapeze artist flying through the air, legs everywhere, skirt round my waist, tops of stockings and suspenders showing. Then the noise of the chair crashing to the ground; next minute, charging to my rescue were all these men. I should have been flattered, but instead I was totally embarrassed. All I could do was laugh, probably with embarrassment. That was the first of many.

While I was working here, I spent most of my free time with my Friend from school and although I no longer went to the pictures on a Friday with my parents like I had done as a child, I still went to the cinema, but now with my friend. We would go to the Lido at West Ealing every Saturday evening regardless of what film was on, and would sit about four rows from the front on the right hand side. We would never dream of sitting anywhere else – funny thing is, I can't remember why.

We had been doing this for a while and then one week three boys were shown to the empty seats next to us, my friend and I looked at them and then at each other. We didn't need to say a word we were both thinking the same thing: we couldn't wait for the lights to come on during the interval so we could see what they looked like. I can't remember how the conversation started but straight away we were talking to each other.

Saturdays now had a different meaning for me. It was the day I would meet these new friends, and they were boys. I would take extra care in choosing what to wear, to make sure my makeup was just right, and the seams of my stockings were straight. Then one Saturday they brought another friend with them; he had on a brown suit that looked too big for him. He also had a bandage on his hand and told us he had burnt it at work. Nothing drew me to him except that he was good looking.

The following week he came, and this time asked if he could sit next to me. I said yes, but was really not interested in him, so the next week before my friend and I went to the cinema I said I would sit next to the wall then she was to sit next to me and for her not to move if he turned up. Guess what she did. So again he sat next to me. At the end of the evening he asked if he could walk me home, and even though I did not want him to, I said yes. .

Part 3.

NEW EMOTIONS

I arranged to meet him the following week in the cinema, and again he took me home. He asked if he could see me one evening and I said yes. Soon we were meeting two or three times a week, and I was now beginning to look forward to spending more time with him, sometimes going for walks, other times to the pictures. When I look back living in an area were there were four cinemas - the Walpole, Forum, Lido and Palladium - there were plenty of films to choose from. Here I will give you a little history on each of these cinemas.

The Walpole was in Bond Street in Ealing, and was built in 1912, but demolished in 1981. The Forum, built alongside the Uxbridge Road at Ealing, was designed by John Stanley Beard, who had earlier designed the Walpole. The old cinema organ which was once played there is now used in the chapel at Wormwood Scrubs Prison. The Lido was built in West Ealing, and is at this time (2007) being demolished; it was never really popular and was once voted the worst cinema in the country. The Palladium, also along side the Uxbridge Road and not far from Ealing Broadway Station, was built in 1910 and demolished in 1958 - now replaced by W.H. Smith.

To me there was always something special about the Palladium, which stood out from the others, not only by the design of the building, but the Montague Ballroom, which was situated at the back - where my friend and I had tried so often to get into the dancehall while we were still at school. How many times had we fooled the doorman I wonder, or maybe we never fooled him at all.

I can still see the plush carpet in the foyer and the swing doors which led to the ballroom. I hear the music playing and feel the beating of my heart as I wait for the voice that says 'do you want to dance?' Occasionally we would get a 65 bus to Richmond or Kew in Surrey. At Richmond we would spend our time walking along the river, watching the boats going up and down, seeing the swans and ducks being fed by children throwing bread into the water or holding it in their hand, hearing their laughter and screams as each bird would come and reach for the treat that would be theirs. Hands being pulled away quickly in case they grabbed tiny fingers. Parents standing by, laughing but anxious. Then children's laughter turning to tears when the bread had all gone and it was time to go.

When we went to Kew we would visit the gardens. The real name for them is the Royal Botanic Gardens, but is mainly known as Kew Gardens; it was first started in the 1700s and has gradually been added to over the years. Plants from all over the world are grown here, both common and exotic; if you ever have a chance to go, you should, as it is well worth a visit. When I went as a child with Mum and Dad, we would pay a penny each to go in; this we would put in a turnstile and then hear it creak as it turned (probably needed oiling). I don't expect it's a penny any more. My sister and I would run and play on the grass, doing cartwheels, seeing who could do the most before stopping. Mum would bring a picnic and we would sit, eat sandwiches and drink lemonade. I remember having our photo taken with a box like camera which was called a Brownie. I can see Dad now trying to change the film with his coat over his head so as not to let the light in, hoping the film would not be exposed before he had time to roll it up and then trying to replace it with another roll of film - the coat still over his head still trying not to let the light in (happy days). But now going with **him**, was different, I no longer did cartwheels, this time I held hands.

To cross over the river at Kew there is a large bridge which was built about hundred and twenty years ago, and one of the interesting points about this area is that it is the site of Julius Caesar's first battle on British soil. (By the way the Brits lost the battle.) Now there are no Roman Legions crossing the river, just Legions of cars crossing a bridge. When you looked over the side of the bridge there was a small fun fair where we would sometimes go. A few years later it was taken away, sad really. Behind the fair was a public house called 'The Boathouse,' but I will tell you about that later.

Those long summer nights were so special, getting to know each other learning, each other's likes and dislikes, and talking about our families. There is something about courting that is different from any other time in your life He told me he was an apprentice plumber and liked his job very much. I did wonder at the time why any one would want to be a plumber, but I suppose they do have their uses, especially when you have a burst pipe or you need the washer on your tap changed. He was very talkative, so this made it easy for me, as there were not too many silences of not knowing what to say next

He spoke often about his Mum and Dad and soon said he wanted me to meet them. They lived in a council house in Southall, Middlesex. In the front garden there was a cherry tree, and in the spring it was always covered in blossom. I can't remember whether it was just a flowering cherry or a fruit tree, but I do know it was the only house in his road with a tree in the front garden.

As you went into the house there was a small passage with a door that led into a living room, which then led to a kitchen at the back of the house. Upstairs were two bedrooms and a bathroom. Under the front window in the living room was a large table where his Mum would sit for hours looking out onto the road, watching everything and every one. I never understood why she did this, but soon learnt that she rarely went out during the day, and it was his Dad who did most of the shopping, so the only time she seemed to spend away from the house was when she went to the working men's club.

I remember her as a small stocky woman who always seemed to

have her hair in curlers, using pipe cleaners to curl her hair. All day she would walk around the house with these curled close to her head.

His Dad too was short and stocky and a memory I have of him is cutting his toenails which were so strong they could not be cut with scissors so he would go to his tool box, get a large file, put his foot on a chair and file away. (Funny the things you remember.)

I learnt that his Dad had always worked for the railway as an engine driver. I can see him now in his overalls, his cap on his head and a bag swung across his shoulders. I'm not sure what was in his bag, probably his sandwiches. Whether his Mum had ever been out to work I am not sure, but I don't remember her ever mentioning anything to me. He had two brothers who were much older than him, but they no longer lived at home as they were both married, the oldest one having a young daughter.

There are three things that mainly stand out in my memory about his home. First the black range, or kitchen stove they had in their living room. It consisted of a small built-in fire and at the side of this was an oven. It was built in one piece, and his Mum would always have a kettle filled with water sitting on the top. I remember the tea always tasting stewed when she used the water from the kettle. I never mentioned this, but was always glad when I had got to the bottom of the cup, and I never asked for more.

The second thing I remember is that there was no electricity in the house - instead there lighting was gas. I never realised that people still had their homes lit this way, so was most surprised. I can see them now, turning the tap at the side of the light to let the gas through. A lighted match would be put close to the little bulb, called a mantle, being careful not to touch it as they could break very easily, and then hear the pop as the gas would ignite and come to life. Because I had grown up with electricity, all the electrical items I had in my home I took for granted, so when I realised that even to listen to the wireless (that's what a radio used to be called), they had to have one that was especially adapted to a battery, I was even more surprised. Also, as she was unable to have an electric iron, she would use in stead a flat iron which was heated by putting on top of a gas flame on the cooker. When hot enough, she would pick it up with a cloth and then iron till it cooled, then use a second one that was heating up while she was doing this.

The third thing that stands out in my memory is the piano that took pride of place in their living room. His Mum was the only one able to play, but I don't think she did this very often.

The back garden was very long and narrow where his Dad had grown vegetables, and at one time, kept chickens. That last sentence has reminded me of a story he told me. Years ago if you had household items you no longer needed, you would not get in touch with the Council like you do today for them to dispose of. Instead, there were rag and bone men who came round the streets on a horse and cart collecting all the items you no longer wanted. They would come down the street shouting out "Rag and Bone" or "any old iron" in a language you could hardly understand, but even from inside your house you would always be able to hear them. For the rags or items you gave them, they would give you money or a chick, and sometimes a goldfish. He had heard the rag and bone man coming down the street and had asked his Mum for some old items to take out, hoping to get a goldfish, but because he had a garden he was given a chick. He took it home and looked after it till it became a fine looking cockerel. He said it would follow his Mum all through the house, so soon became a family pet. His older brother, who was in the army at this time, was coming home on leave; you've guessed it; his Mum and Dad decided to have a chicken dinner. The sad conclusion to this story is that no one was able to eat their food, not even his brother when he was told the story behind his chicken dinner.

Standing in the corner of the garden was a mangle for squeezing water from the clothes after they had been washed. It had a frame made of iron, with two big wooden rollers and a handle on the side which you would turn to make the rollers go round. You would then put the wet clothes up to the rollers, being careful not to get your fingers caught as you turned the handle. The clothes would then come out flat on the other side and you had to catch them before they fell to the ground. Sometimes you would put a bowl there hoping they would fall into that. Even in the pouring rain you would stand and ring the clothes, glad we don't have to do that anymore; this progress I agree with.

The first time I met his Mum and Dad was when he took me to the working men's club. I was not sure what to expect as I had never been to one before. I learnt that much of his young childhood had been spent going there with his parents. Most nights he would fall asleep, and then he would be carried home on his Dad's shoulders. He did tell me one story that he would repeat many times over the years. As he got older he was allowed to go over the park on his own. This time he had gone with his friends, and when the park had closed, he had made his way home wanting to go to bed, but when he got there his Mum and Dad were still down the club. Not having a key to the front door he was unable to get in, so he tried to force the front window and broke it. Not a happy family that night.

When he got older he too became a member of the club and because they had a snooker room, became a frequent visitor. He would spend much of his free time playing this game with his mates and other members, even betting money. He must have been very good as sometimes he would win more than his week's wages.

We would go to the club most Saturdays, and I would sit with his Mum and Dad, drinking lemonade and talking. I can't remember what we spoke about, but because I fitted into their life style, they accepted me.

As I got to know his brothers and there families I would be invited with him to their homes. They would always make me feel welcome, and so I felt I was becoming part of his family. On occasion if we were going somewhere special, we would take his niece with us. She was a lovely little girl with long blond hair and always polite. I remember taking her to a pantomime at Chiswick Empire. I can see her now with ice cream dripping down her chin but too excited to notice.

Chiswick Empire - it's sad that you will never be able to see or visit this Theatre. It was built on Chiswick High Street by Frank Matcham, and opened on the 2nd of September 1912, but demolished in 1959. I would go there often and see shows of all types, from comedy to ballet, musicals to ice shows. Many great artists appeared there over the years such as Julie Andrews, Laurel and Hardy, Vivien Leigh, James Mason and Dirk Bogarde, to name but a few. I know you probably have never herd of most of these people, but we would queue to see them, just as you do when you know that your favourite group is in town. What did they replace it with? An office building!

It was quite a while before he met my Mum and Dad, even though he would see me home on the nights we went out. I did not take him to meet them straight away because I wanted to be sure of how I felt about him, but when they finally met, Mum liked him; Dad never said much. Now he was being invited to tea and being made to feel one of the family and I was growing more fond of him. When we were together he always wanted to stay those extra five minuets, so he would often miss his last bus home and have to walk, which would take ages. So he decided to use his bike and would cycle in all weathers; Mum was always nagging him because he never seamed to wear enough clothes, especially when it was bitter cold. One of her favourite sayings to him was "where's your tie?" Because Dad never went out without wearing a tie, they both felt that this was the right way to dress, but he never took any notice. I do remember that one day for a joke he turned up with a very bright tie on, it had a very colourful peacock painted on the front, in he walked, with a massive grin on his face. I don't think they made a remark about a tie again, but we all had a good laugh that day.

Visiting the club as often as I did I began to meet different people, amongst them was a family who had been friends with his family for many years. They had a daughter who he had grown up with. I did get the impression that both families had hoped that one day they would marry. He said he had never courted her, as he had no feelings for her in that way; she was always nice to me, so I never felt any jealousy towards her.

Now the weeks turned into months, and the road I was taking was a happy one. I was 16 and he was 17, and thought that life could only get better. Even so, I did not expect the question he asked me. It was a Saturday night and we had been to the club. The evening had gone well, we had laughed and joked, he had played snooker with his mates, and now he was taking me home. We were sitting upstairs on a 607 bus and talking about the evening, when he suddenly asked me to marry him. At first I thought that I had heard wrong, so I asked him to repeat what he had said. I know you will think that 16 is young, but then it was normal for girls to leave school and marry very soon after; your 'career' was getting married and raising a family. Today girls have so much more opportunity, going to collage to further their education and then to make a career in jobs that we could only dream about.

So here I am sitting upstairs on a 607 bus thinking 'how do I answer this?' Do I want to marry this boy? Do I even want to marry? By the time we got off the bus I knew my answer was going to be yes. He said he had been giving money each week to his brother to save for him, so he could buy me an engagement ring. I don't think it crossed my mind what our parents would say, we just enjoyed the moment. When we did tell them, they did not seem surprised.

By now, my outlook changed, I began to dream of weddings and a home of my own. I started collecting items for my bottom draw, it all became very exciting. But wait a minute - a bottom draw? What it that, I hear you say, so I will explain. It's a very old fashioned custom that goes back a long way. In most bedrooms one piece of furniture would always be a chest of draws and when the girl had become engaged to be married she would empty the bottom draw of the chest and this would be gradually filled with lots of items that were bought during the period of the engagement. They would be items such as towels, dusters, knives and forks; in fact, anything that would fit into it. I think it was always the bottom draw because it is nearly always the deepest, so therefore more could be put into it. We never set a date to get married as we earned so little money between us; we knew it would take time to save for the things we wanted, but we did not mind, we were happy and looked forward to the future.

Even though the war had been over for about nine years, boys of 18 were still drafted into the forces and would have to serve their country for two years. Those who had an apprenticeship, which normally lasted from the age of fifteen to twenty-one, did not have to go until they finished their course. So as an Apprentice Plumber, he still had a few years before he would be called up. Even so, our future together looked good and it seemed as if nothing could spoil the roads that we were about to take together. We talked about things we would do, of the places we would go. What we would be doing in ten years time (that seemed so far ahead). Everything looked so rosy. But how naive can we be? Because of one wrong act, my life would go down a different road.

It was a Saturday night and we were going to a dance that was being held at the club. I took special care in choosing what to wear and was really excited at the thought of dancing. I had arranged to meet him at the club. When I got there, all his friends and family had arrived and the hall was packed; everyone, it seemed, wanted to enjoy the dance. What a good time we were having, nothing, it seemed, could spoil the evening. We were together, and I was happy.

We had just danced and the music had finished and while we were waiting for the next tune to start, across the dance floor walking towards us was the daughter of his family's friends. Can I have the next dance? she asked, looking straight at him (suddenly I have become invisible). I did not mind him dancing with her, as he had said he had no special feelings for her, she was just his friend. So I went back and sat with his Mum, expecting him to leave her when the dance had finished. But the music started again and they were still dancing; now I was only half listening to what his Mum was saying to me, as I was watching them. They were dancing very close and she had her arms around his neck. I could see them talking to each other and he was enjoying it. Now what started to go through my mind was maybe there was more to their friendship than he had said. So, being a 16-year old with no real experience of life, and not knowing how to handle the situation, I got up from my chair, grabbed my coat, said good night to his Mum and left.

I started to walk to the bus stop, hoping he would come after me, not walking too fast so he would catch me up, praying the bus would not come too soon, and still not believing what had happened. What had I done? Had I overreacted? Should I have just ignored it? All these thoughts were going through my mind, and then there he was, but I never heard the words that I was hopping to hear; instead he said the engagement was off and it was all over. I could not believe what I was hearing; only a few hours earlier we had been talking about our future, of all the things we were going to do and the places we were going to go. He had told me he loved me and I had believed him. I thought you loved me, I said, but he turned and walked away.

Now I wanted the bus to come, I could not get home quick enough. When Mum and Dad saw me, they knew something was wrong, but they never said a word. I went straight to bed and cried in my pillow. All week I waited for a ring at the door bell or a letter in the post, hoping he had changed his mind, hoping he was missing me as much as I was missing him. I waited and waited, but he never got in touch. By the following week I could not bear it any longer; I had not heard from him and I missed him. I decided that if he would not come to me, I would go to him.

I knew what time he would be home from work and arrived just before him. His Mum and Dad were pleased to see me, but they did not mention what had happened. When he walked in they left us to talk. He said he was surprised I had come to see him, but he had not changed his mind and the engagement was still off. He said there had been a row with his older brother after I had left the club and when he had got home; there had been another argument with his Mum and Dad. I asked if he had seen his friend's daughter since that night, and he said no. So I had over reacted and lost it all. He said that he had been given back the money his brother had saved for him and things were still not right between them. When we finished talking he took me home, but I don't think we spoke much, as there was nothing left to say.

So now it was back to meeting my friend on a Saturday and going to the pictures with her, secretly hoping that he would turn up and it would be like it was before.

It was about four weeks later when I saw him next. I had been shopping in West Ealing and was on my way home. When I saw him walking towards me, my stomach turned - what was I going to say to him? What would he say to me? Would he say he had missed me and wanted us to be together again? So many thoughts were going through my mind in so little time. But all he said was Hallo asked how I was and then he was gone. When I got home I cried, and Mum held me close. Dad walked in and asked what was wrong, and I can still hear Mum whisper 'she's just seen him.'

I had accepted that it really was all over between us, when to my surprise I received a letter, asking me to meet him in the Lido cinema the following Saturday afternoon. What did he want? I kept asking myself. Did he now regret what had happened, and did he want to start again? I was not even sure if I wanted to see him. I was beginning to feel better, and did not want to go through all the pain again. I talked it over with my friend at work; she said I should go, but I was still not sure. When I asked Mum and Dad what I should do, they said I must decide for myself. Then I reasoned that if I did meet him, I might not have the same feelings as before and that would make it easier for me (did I really believe that?).

I counted the days till Saturday, not sure of what was going to happen. I must not be the first to arrive, I must not seem too eager, I kept saying to myself. But I did get there first and waited, wondering if he would turn up.

It was all very polite to start with; I think he was as nervous as I was. He had not been in the cinema long when he suggested that we leave and go for a walk. What was he going to say? So many things were going through my mind. But I did not expect the words that he said. He stopped, then turned me to face him and said 'I've signed on and I'm going in the Army' for twenty two years.

Had I heard right? Did he say that he was going in the Army? Did he say **twenty two years**? This had not been the road we had mapped out for ourselves. I was devastated. I could not believe what he had just told me. Why? I said, as I began to cry, I don't want you to go away. I loved him, and wanted him to stay with me.

He told me that things had become very difficult at home since the Saturday we had broken up and so felt it was time for him to leave, and the obvious place to go he said, was the Army. He had signed on for twenty two years, but there was a three year option which would give him leeway to change his mind if he did not want to make the Army a career. But I still could not believe what he was telling me, and it had all stemmed from that one Saturday night and the decision I had made. He asked if I would write to him, but there was no mention of our engagement. I did wonder whether he had just got in touch with me for someone to write to, but I kept quiet, afraid of the answer.

Now all I could think of was him going away. He said his training period was six weeks, and then most likely he would be sent abroad, and as he had broken his apprenticeship, he could continue this in the Army. He sounded very excited, as there was a new life stretching out in front of him; but in all his excitement, I felt he never gave much thought of how his going away would affect me.

I can't remember what happened during those next few weeks waiting for him to leave. I only see myself standing on Ealing Broadway Station waiting for the train that would take him away, waving goodbye, and me in tears; then the platform guard coming up and asking if I was OK. I told the guard my story and he said it's only six weeks, which will soon go.

Now I began to look forward to the postman coming every day. I would run down to the door when I heard him, always hoping to find a letter on the doormat, and if one was not there, would rush home from work each evening hoping it might have been delivered by second post. Sometimes Dad would hide them in all different places for me to find, so it became a game of "find the letter". But the joy I felt when I saw the envelope with my name on the front and all the writing on the back, even before I opened the envelope there in big letters S.W.A.L.K. which stood for "Sealed With A Loving Kiss" and then kisses printed all round was immense.

The six weeks did go much quicker than I expected and soon he was standing at my door looking like a soldier in his khaki uniform. He stood very proud and was eager to tell me all about this new life of being a soldier in The Royal Engineers.

He began to tell me of the things he had done over the past six weeks, of all the training, including all the marching. Now that the training was over he had been given a weekend pass, and we had to make the most of it, as he was not sure when he would be home again.

But there was a surprise in store, because the Army had taken over his apprenticeship he was not going to be sent overseas straight away. This meant that we were able to see each other most weekends. He would go home first, then come round to me, spend a little time with Mum and Dad, and then we would go back to his home, and always end up going to the club. At the same time he went into the army his friends went too, though not in the same regiment.

I can't say that I enjoyed the next few months, always wondering if he would be coming home at the weekend, sometimes planning what we would do, and then to be let down because he was unable to get a weekend pass. The Sunday mornings he was home, he would spend ironing his uniform; I would sit on a chair in his kitchen and watch him pressing away using a damp cloth or brown paper for what seemed ages, making sure his uniform looked perfect. Next he would clean his boots. He would open a tin of black boot polish, and then into the lid he would pour water. He would dip a rag first into the water and then onto the polish and this he would rub into his boots going round and round until they shone. Sometimes he would spit on the boot; this is where the saying 'Spit and Polish' comes from. We would talk and laugh while I watched in amazement at the pride he took in doing this. As I remember, I can see him and my heart weighs heavy.

During this time I would visit his Mum and Dad and later asked her if she would like to go to the   cinema. Soon it became a regular weekly outing. I was very surprised that she did this, as I had never known her to go to the cinema before.

I can't remember how long it was before he came home and told me that he was being shipped abroad. He said he was going to Singapore and did not know how long he would be away, but thought it would be at least two years. As you can imagine I was upset about this, but there was nothing I could do, so I tried to remain cheerful.

It was our last time together, the days had gone so fast and I still could not believe that I would not see him for such a long time. It was Friday night and he was leaving on Sunday, we had been for one of our many walks, and the silences between us had grown longer. Now the silence was broken, and he was telling me he loved me, and gave me an engagement ring. He wanted me to wait for him, and said we would be married when he got home.

But this time I did not give him an answer straight away; I would think about it, I said, and let him know the following day. Once again I began to question what I should do. He was going to be away for at least two years; his life was going to be a new adventure, and time for him would go fast. But for me, all I could see was doing the same things I had always done, so time would not go fast for me. .

I could not sleep that night; questions were going round and round in my mind. When I asked Mum and Dad what I should do, Dad said it would not be good to tie myself down by becoming engaged. He said our feelings for each other could change in two years, but the time separated would give us both a chance to be sure of what we wanted.

When he came to see me the following day I told him I loved him, but did not think it a good idea to get engaged, giving him the reasons why I felt this way. We could write to each other I said, and make a decision about an engagement when he came home. He agreed to this, but still wanted me to have the ring. .

That last evening was not a good time; I kept thinking what will I do for the next two years. Little did I know that he was not the only one whose life on taking a new road was going to be filled with adventures.

Part 4.

MY TIME

I wish I could remember the name of the station where we said our last goodbye, then maybe you could go there and let your imagination work for you, but I can't. I only see myself walking quickly alongside him while making our way to the train. There are people everywhere going about their business, all going down their own roads. I know they are there, but I don't see them, and I am not concerned about the roads they are taking.

I can see him now leaning out of the window of the train, and I can tell by the look on his face that he doesn't know what to say to me. All I know is that I don't want him to go. He's saying something about writing, but all I hear is the guard calling out 'Mind the Doors' and the sound of a whistle. Soon the train begins to move; I run alongside trying to keep up, but I can't. What will I do now? I say to myself as I stand and watch as the train disappears into the distance.

Several months have gone by, and I am still doing the same things and going to the same places. Except I now have a new job. I am working in a typing pool with lots of other girls. The office is large, with rows of desks and the sound of typewriters banging away, and with a supervisor who sits at the end of the room watching all that we do (I wonder why it reminds me of school). I go to the cinema, shop in West Ealing, and look forward to his letters from Singapore. So as I said, all is just the same - except for the postmark on the envelope. I should have added visiting his parents on the list, but I don't see them anymore, as one of his letters tell me his Mum has written to him and said that I am seeing other boys. I don't know why she did this as at the time, because it was not true. But he said he wrote back telling her that I must get on with my life, just as he is. (He never did ask me if it was true.) His letters tell me he is having a great time, and I am glad for him, but I begin to wonder, will there be any great times for me? Or perhaps I'm just feeling sorry for myself.

Even though I don't like working in the typing pool I stay because the firm is close to home and easy for me to get to. I get the 65 Bus to the Dome Garage on The Great West Road in Brentford, and then it's just a five minute walk. Providing I never have to wait too long for the bus, it only takes me about twenty minuets to get there.

It was just another day at the office when I overheard the girls talking; one of them was saying she wanted to go to a holiday camp for her holiday and was looking for someone to go with her. As no one seemed to be interested in going, without thinking, I said I would love to go. A 'holiday camp,' I hear you say - that's not very exciting, but there were no cheap air fares to exotic places then. For most people, it was a week or a fortnight (if you were lucky) once a year at an English seaside resort, and as I had never been away from home on my own, and certainly not on holiday, the thought of doing this was exciting.

I began saving as much as I could and now was counting days for a different reason. I don't know what I expected, but when I got off the train at Clacton-on-Sea, I felt the excitement of independence. The camp was situated close to the beach and the first thing I noticed was the Fun Fair, especially the Big Wheel, which towered above the rest of the amusements. This only added to my excitement. I was almost 17, and this was my first holiday on my own; I intended to make the most of it. When we arrived at the camp we were given keys to a two bedroom chalet, which consisted of bunk beds a small wardrobe, chest of draws and a sink. For our meals there was a communal dining room.

Each morning we were woken by the sound of what seemed like a few notes being played on a xylophone, and then a voice coming from a sound system on the camp which said 'Morning Campers,' telling us that breakfast would soon be served in the dining room. After breakfast we would either join in the camp entertainment or make our own fun. Some days were spent sunbathing on the beach and because the beaches were so crowded then; you had to search for a space to sit. Today most people go abroad for their holidays and because of this, English seaside resorts are dying, which is so sad. Other times we walked into town, looking around the shops and the arcades. I can picture it now: hot sunny days, eating candy floss with a hat on my head which had written across the brim 'Kiss me Quick" (nobody did though). We strolled along the pier which stretched out into the sea hoping, as I walked, that it would not collapse. Walking to the end, but glad when I made my way back to the part where I could no longer see the sea staring at me through the wooden boards under my feet. Clacton pier is really old. It was constructed and opened to the public in 1871, so perhaps it was a good thing I never knew that then (it still stands today).

Each day brought something new which I enjoyed to the full, but the evenings were something special, and I looked forward to them the most. This was because a new type of dancing was beginning; it was called Rock and Roll, or Jiving. It first started in America and had soon made its way across the water to us. The tempo of music had changed. No longer were we listening to people like Frank Sinatra, Dean Martin or Perry Como (I doubt you will know who they were); instead it was Tommy Steal, Little Richard, Bill Haley and Elvis Presley, who later became known as "The King:" (you probably won't know these either). It was here in the ballroom that I learnt to Rock and Roll, and as each day passed I began to enjoy my independence and to realise there was a different life to be had from the one I was so used to.

Soon the week that had stretched out in front of me had come to an end, and it was time to return home. I tried to settle back into my routine, but some how things were not the same. I no longer wanted to work at a job I did not like, or spend most of my free time at the cinema. I realised that if I wanted to take a different road than the one I was taking, I would have to do something about it myself.

I did not mention what my intentions were to Mum and Dad because I knew that they would not approve, and besides, I had to make sure that I had a job to go to first. I can see myself now, all nervous thinking about the telephone call I was about to make. Half of me wanting to keep walking to the telephone box, and the other half wanting to turn around and go back home. But I kept walking and soon was talking to the telephone operator at the Holiday Camp and was asking if they had any job vacancies. She said they had, and then gave me the choice of either waitressing or being a chalet maid, which basically meant being a chalet cleaner. I said that I preferred the chalet maid. I can't remember why I chose this, but I must have had my reasons at the time. Straight away they gave me a date to start. Now I had to go home and tell Mum and Dad. This I was not looking forward too, but I was determined that no matter what they said nothing was going to stop me.

Mum cried; Dad kept pacing back and forth, going out into the scullery and back again. They gave me all the reasons why I should not go. It's too dangerous. You have never been on your own. It's so far away. We don't want you to go. But I did not listen; all I could see in front of me was a new road, and I wanted to take it.

Home had now become a very hard place to be; there was no longer any laughter and the joy I had always felt was gone. Mum was not singing like she always did, and Dad was very quiet. I knew it was my fault, but I was still determined to do what I had set my mind to. I have often wondered, as I look back over my years, what has driven me to deal with the things that have gone on in my life, and as I write all this down, it has shown that I have a drive and determination, and without it, I am sure I would have crumbled many times. So here I am, my case packed and in a taxi taking me to Ealing Broadway station, glad that Mum and Dad are at work, which makes leaving a lot easier. I am on my way to take a new road, and I can't wait.

When I arrived at the camp I went to the personnel office and filled out an application form and then was shown to the place I was to lodge. It was a large bungalow or so it seemed; opposite the camp, and from the outside looked most inviting. As we walked I was told that my meals would be in the staff canteen which I would find on the camp, and I was to start work the following morning. I can't remember the hours I had to work, but I do remember that I had one or two afternoons off in the week. The following morning I was to go first to the personnel office and then a member of staff would take me to my department. I am not sure if there were many do's and don'ts, except one and that was once staff had finished their day's work they were not allowed back on the chalet lines. I never gave this much thought as I had no intention at the time of doing this.

The room I was shown too was quit big and had in it several single and bunk beds. It reminded me of films I had seen of children in dormitories when they had been sent away to a boarding school or to a work house. There was nothing at all homey or inviting about it, even though it was clean and tidy (this should have given me some clues). My heart sank - the one thing I had not thought about before leaving home was what sort of accommodation I would be living in. Suddenly a doubt came into my mind - should I have come? Because I felt this way, I did not bother to unpack my suitcase; I just took out my pyjamas and left them on the bed to let the other people in the room know I was there. Then, pushing my suitcase under the bed, decided to go back to the camp and go to the places I had been to while on holiday, hoping this would make me feel better. But the excitement I had during my holiday was not there.

Soon it was time to find my way to the staff canteen. I can see myself now, standing in the queue, not knowing what to do, watching and hoping I get it right. I feel as if every one is looking at me as I am the new girl, but of course this is not true. While I queue for my food, which I have to say looks very good, I look around and the atmosphere is very lively. People are laughing and talking and enjoying each other's company, but I feel out of place and very alone. After eating I make my way back to my lodgings. There I sit on my bed, waiting for another member of staff to turn up, but nobody does. I then realise why the room is so tidy. I am the only one staying there.

The following morning after breakfast I was shown by a member of staff to a large cupboard which was situated on the end of one of the chalet lines. It contained brooms, buckets, and cloths, all the items that were needed to clean the chalets. I was told to make the beds each day and do a general clean. Also once a week I was to polish the wooden floors. This would consist of filling a bucket with a thick brown substance which was thrown to the floor with a stick and then with a cloth on the end of a broom, was rubbed into the wood. After that another cloth was put on the broom, this time for buffing to make the wood shine. I was given a green overall and a bunch of keys and then taken to the chalet line that would be mine. It consisted of 16 chalets, each having two sets of bunk beds. I was told that the campers who occupied my chalets were boys, except at the height of the season, when I would probably have families. I found out later that they did not normally put boys and girls on the same chalet lines unless the lines allocated to each were full.

It had been nearly two weeks since I had arrived at the camp, and loneliness was beginning to take over. I was missing home and the warmth of my family and because they had not moved anyone else into the room I was staying in, this did not help. I think at this time I could have caught the first train home, but I was determined to stay for a while longer, hoping things would get better. I wrote home telling Mum and Dad that all was well and I had settled in and was enjoying my job. How could I tell them how things really were and how lonely I felt? But by the end of the second week I began to get used to going to the canteen, and soon was talking with different people and making new friends. They had come from all parts of the country, starting work at the beginning of the holiday season, as the camp did not stay open all year round; for many, it was not their first time of working there.   They said because they enjoyed the atmosphere they came back year after year. Hearing this cheered me up; perhaps things would get better after all I thought.

I began to enjoy going to the camp each day, and would often spend time talking to the boys who stayed in my chalets. They would tell me about the places where they lived and the life they had left behind for a short time; I was beginning to feel glad that I had not given in to my feelings and returned home. The only downside was my accommodation. I was still on my own in the room, and had not seen any one else in the bungalow since I had moved in, so at times I still felt very lonely. Then one morning before I started work I was called into the personnel office and told I would be moving to another hotel which was situated on the seafront a little distance away from the camp, and because they did not want us to rely on public transport, a camp bus was used and would travel at set times during the day. How pleased I was even though I was not sure what to expect.

As I stood and looked at the hotel from the outside I knew that I was going to enjoy living there, as it was much larger than the bungalow, and very elegant. I felt that my room was going to be some place special, with lots of space and a comfortable bed - a place that I could call home. As I went into the entrance there was a little kiosk and sitting in it was a staff member who looked after the hotel. She took me through a large sitting room which was filled with chairs, couches and small tables, but as it was during the day there were only a few people in there. How my hopes were raised when I saw how neat and clean everything was; I knew I was going to like it here! We made our way upstairs where I was shown into my room, but what a shock I got - it was nothing like what I had imagined. The room was very small, yet still they had managed to put into it bunk beds, a dressing table, small wardrobe and a sink, which left hardly any room to move around in. I noticed it was already occupied, but what stood out most was that the room was so untidy; there were clothes thrown everywhere. As I was trying to take it all in, I was thinking that perhaps the bungalow wasn't so bad after all. I don't remember much about the girl I shared with, as I didn't see her very often since her working hours were different from mine. But even though she now had a roommate, she never did get any tidier.

Just before I had left home I decided to go to the hairdresser, as I wanted to look my best for my new job, and they had suggested that I have my hair permed. Thinking that they knew best, I took their advice - much to my regret! I no longer looked as I did when I came out of the hairdresser - my hair now looked like a frizzy ball, and even though I had tried everything to make it look better, it still looked like a frizzy ball. Not long after I started working at the camp, I noticed that many of the girls had dyed their hair blond, so now my mind was beginning to work overtime. I began to wonder what I would look like as a blond and maybe it would help with the frizz.

On my next afternoon off I went into town and bought a peroxide hair dye. Before long I had changed from a brunet into a yellow blond, but yellow was not the intention. So back to town I go to buy another hair dye and do it all over again, never thinking it might be too much too soon. Now I really **was** a blond, but the frizz was still there; so back to town I go, but this time to the hairdresser, where I have my hair cut really short, asking for a D.A. (short for Ducks Arse), which was a very popular hair style at the time. When I got back to my room I washed my hair then set it in the style of the cut, and when I looked in the mirror I no longer saw the girl who only weeks ago had lived in a narrow world, but a new one who had now become a very different person. Not only had I changed my hair, but with it, my outlook as well.

I no longer saw work as a drudge as I had done before; now it was a place I wanted to be. I looked forward to each day knowing it would bring with it something new. I remember mornings that were bright and sunny, not catching the bus to the camp, but instead walking with my friends along the beach holding my shoes in my hand and feeling the sand beneath my feet. It was the fifties - the time of the Teddy Boys and Rock and Roll, and I was part of it.

Because most campers stayed for just one week, no sooner did I get used to them then they were gone and new ones had replaced them. The work was not easy, as there were so many beds to make each day, and boys are not the most tidy! I would get to each chalet, rattle my bunch of keys, then bang on the door calling out "it's the Chalet maid," hoping that they would be out of bed by the time I got there. The funny thing was that at the beginning of there week they would be up and out early in the morning, but as the days went by, I would find some still in their bed, getting over the night before, and others who's beds had not been slept in at all. But Saturday was the hardest day of the week, as beds would have to be stripped and sheets changed for the new guests - besides making sure the chalets were clean - so no chalet maid looked forward to Saturdays, especially if it rained. I think it was the polishing of the floors I disliked the most. I would end up getting more polish on me than the floor, and by the time I had finished I was really tired and glad when my work day had come to an end.

One of the best parts of working at a holiday camp is that you are able to use many of the amenities. After I had my evening meal I would get the bus back to the hotel, wash my hair choose, what to wear, put my makeup on, and go back to the camp and meet up with my friends. First we would go to a bar called 'The Jolly Roger.' We would listen to each other telling stories about the day, never believing that the antics of people could be so funny, or listening to the skiffle band that was playing on the small stage at the end of the bar.

I don't suppose you have herd of skiffle. This was music that preceded Rock and Roll and was popular especially among teenagers as they began to form there own bands and, as they could not afford expensive instruments, would make their own. These consisted of a wash board which was played by putting thimbles on your fingers and then tapping or sliding up and down the board; a tea chest with a broom handle put inside, on which had string tied each end then plucked, and a Kazoo, which you blew into.

Each day that passed I was beginning to feel surer of myself; no longer did I feel like the person on the outside that everyone was staring at. I was now growing up fast I was seeing my world through different eyes. I began spending time with the boy campers, not only while I was cleaning their chalets, but after my work day had finished. I would sometimes meet them in the Jolly Roger or at the dance hall later in the evening. I remember one time I had arranged to meet my friends in the Jolly Roger and had been late getting there; by the time I arrived they had made friends with some of the campers. The only chair that was vacant was next to one of the boys, so I spent much of the time just talking to him. He asked me what I was doing later, and I said that my friends and I would be going to the dance hall, so he asked if he could come with me, and I said ok. When it was time to leave I stood up and so did he. I am five foot four inches tall in bare feet, so with my stiletto heel shoes this would give me at least another 2 inches, and as I looked at him I think he was as shocked as I was, as even in his shoes he only came up to my shoulder. 'Oh hell' he said; I didn't say a word, but unkind or not, I did not meet him at the dance hall.

Another time that stands out is when I was invited one evening to a meal by one of the campers. He said that he had booked a table for us at a restaurant in the town. I spent ages deciding what to wear, first choosing one thing, and then deciding on another. I was really looking forward to the evening. We met as planned and drove to the restaurant. Once inside I saw tables with fine linen cloths, serviettes and flowers. My coat was taken from me and the chair pulled out by one of the waiters for me to sit on - I had never been treated like this before. While we were eating we talked about all sorts of things. This was something I could get used to, I say to myself. We stayed for a while after we had eaten our meal, then he says 'are you ready to go,' as he stands up and helps me on with my coat. Yes, I say, thanking him for a lovely meal. 'You make your way to the car, I must go to the gent's and then pay the bill' were his next words. I make my way to the door and then stroll to the car; next minute I feel this arm grab me - come on, he says, get to the car. So I run to the car with him, next minute we are driving off. Why are you driving so fast I say? Because we had a free meal he says!

One of the funniest times that stands out in my mind is when, after starting work one Saturday morning, I was walking to the chalet line and noticed that there was something different about one of the trees that lined the rows. I looked and looked again, do I see what I think I see I say to myself. For there in front of me is not a tree just growing leaves, but a tree which overnight has now grown condoms. Pinned to the tree is a large piece of paper with the name 'The Condon Tree' written on it. Someone had a good night last night, I think to myself. I make my way back to the office to tell a supervisor who says "that's a new one." There's going to be a funny story to tell in the Jolly Roger tonight I say to myself.

One of the girls in my circle of friends I found out had come from Southall, and so knew all the places that I did. She said that she was only working at the camp for one season, as she would soon be going to America to live. She had applied for the position of a Nanny and was looking forward to going there in a few months. She was a very jolly person, always laughing, always seeing the funny

69

side of things, and you never knew what she would say next. She was very tall and had long blond hair. She also liked dancing and was very good at it, so this was something we had in common.

If you remember, when I first started this job one of the 'don'ts' was that you were not allowed on the chalet lines after work, but this was one of the don'ts I broke. Often, after the dance hall closed we would sneak back on to the chalet lines with the boys we had met, always feeling clever, because we got away with out getting caught. I can see your eyebrows rising, but you would be wrong - there was no hanky-panky, we just sat and talked and when we laughed we had to do it quietly so we would not disturb the other campers. Many a night my friends and I missed the last camp bus home so would have to walk, but we didn't mind as we had enjoyed ourselves. It was worth it.

Try as I might I can't remember more of the time I spent working at the camp. But I do know it was one of the best times of my life, and if I could go back and do it all over again, I would. The wages weren't great, and my accommodations were poor, but I still loved every minuet of it.

Soon the holiday season was coming to an end, but there was no way I wanted to go back home, as all I could see in front of me was the sort of life I had before. So one evening I put to the girl from Southall the idea of finding a job and flat in Clacton. She was all for this as she too did not want to go home, and as she still had not heard about her overseas job, the idea of staying was something she jumped at.

The only jobs we managed to find were in a wood yard, which wasn't very glamorous, but as the holiday season was at an end and most jobs in seaside resorts finished, we could not be choosy. We would get handfuls of wood that had been cut into pieces about seven inches long, put them into a machine and then tie them together to make bundles. These would then be sold to different shops for people to buy, as homes were still mainly kept warm by means of a fire. After working at the camp and enjoying the life that it had given me, this was such a difference.

I had been working at the wood yard for a few weeks when another person began to work there. He too had worked at the holiday camp, and had been employed in security. He said that he recognised both my friend and me, and then told us how security had known that we had gone back onto the chalet lines after work, but because we had behaved ourselves and given them no trouble, they had not reported us. So you see we weren't as clever as we thought we were.
The flat we found was in the basement of a large house and as far as I can remember it consisted of a sitting room, a bedroom with twin beds, and a kitchen which was well equipped - not that we cooked much. I can't remember how much rent we paid; in fact I can't even remember how we managed to find it.

It was a few months since we had decided to stay in Clacton, and even though I had managed to get a job and a flat, I did not settle as I had thought I would. My job was not like working at the camp, where each day I would look forward to being there. I could not make up my mind whether to stay or go back home, but soon the decision was taken for me. We had decided to go out for a drink one evening after work; there we met several boys who were in the air force. When the pub closed we invited them back to our flat, telling them that they would have to be quiet as there were other people in the house. They decided to bring more drink with them so consequently became very noisy, and so in the end we asked them to leave, but instead of leaving by the front door, they decided to climb through a large window that opened onto the pavement. Why they did this I do not know, but even this they did not do quietly. The following day when we arrived home from work there was a letter waiting for us saying that we had to vacate the flat by week's end.

I had written to Mum and Dad telling them I was staying on in Clacton and had found a flat and another job. So when I arrived on the door step with my suitcase in my hand, Mum and Dad must have known that all was not well. I never told them the reason why I had come home and they never asked. Maybe the sight of me - a blond instead of a brunette on the doorstep, must have been a far bigger shock, but once they got used to it they both said being a blond suited me.

Now once again I was looking for employment, but did not find it easy this time. Employers were reluctant to hire me, as they were not sure if I would leave once the summer holiday season started again. This I could understand. But eventually I did get a job at the Hoover factory in Perivale. I am sure you have heard the name Hoover, mainly for their vacuum cleaners. At one time if you wanted a cleaner it was only Hoover you thought of. In fact, I never realized that the name Hoover was the name of the manufacturer until many years later. The Hoover building once again was built in the Art Deco style. It was built between 1931 and 1935 and consisted of both office buildings and factories. It finally closed in 1980 and was bought by the Tesco food company in 1989. But even though the Hoover factory no longer exists, at least Tesco worked with English Heritage to preserve the building.

This time it was not the office I worked in, but the factory, on one of the many assembly lines. My job was putting together one of the armatures that fitted inside a motor. I am not sure what part they played in the motor - all I know is that I had to connect the wiring to the armature and to keep up with the rest of the girls on the line, as a bonus was paid on top of your wages for each armature that was completed by the assembly line. So the more we completed the more bonus we got.

It was not easy to keep up with them at first as most of the girls had been assembling them for some time, but as I got used to doing them

I became much faster. While we worked, music from loudspeakers played, and everyone sang to the songs that came over the radio; it's quite something to hear songs sung this way, even above the noise from the machines.

As my friend from Southall had not yet heard anything about the time she should leave to go to America we continued to meet up. One of the places we frequented was The Greenford Hotel. This was a large building a few yards from The Iron Bridge and a mental hospital called St. Bernard's, just outside the town of Southall. The Iron Bridge is very well known, as it was built by Brunel, a famous iron bridge engineer more than 150 years ago. St. Bernard's Hospital was formerly the county lunatic asylum; they started building this in 1829 and it was opened in 1831. But the hospital will come into my story a little later.

There is a story behind the naming of the Greenford Hotel and it goes something like this. This hotel and another hotel which was situated on the Greenford Road were constructed at the same time by the same builders, and for obvious reasons, the hotel near the bridge should have been called the Bridge Hotel, but because of a mix-up, the hotel on the Greenford Road was called the Bridge Hotel, where there is not a bridge at all, and you've guessed, it the hotel by the bridge was called the Greenford Hotel and because lots of the furniture and mirrors had already been stamped with the hotels' names on and they had been installed, they decided to leave things as they were. I always think this is quite a funny story and always giggle to myself when I think of it.

I can see us now, sometimes sitting at the bar or at the small tables that were placed around the room. But what stands out the most is the man who entertained us by playing a violin; not just an ordinary violin - he had transformed it so it was connected to the electrics and then to loudspeakers, and because of this, the sound was changed and amplified. I know this does not seem very original today, but to me it was something new - I had never seen or heard this before.

At this time there was no new boy in my life, I had just gone back once again to doing all the things I had previously done before I went away, as I knew I would. But my friend had met a boy and was beginning to see him quite regularly. She told me she was becoming very fond of him and I remember wondering at the time whether she would change her mind about going abroad, but when the time came for her to leave she was so excited about going and I felt her feelings for him would disappear once she settled into her new life,

Soon we were all saying our goodbyes at a leaving party her family had organised for her, and of course there was laughter, and tears, all evening - but still everyone was happy that she was making a new life for herself, and I suppose I admired the courage it took for her to go so far away and to a family she had never met. I remembered how difficult it had been for me to make the decision to leave home, and I was only a couple of hours away by train.

Again I try to remember the things I did with my life at this time, but nothing stands out other than after my friend had gone, I went to the Greenford Hotel a couple of times on my own. But of course going on my own wasn't the same. I did meet a boy there and dated him a couple of times, but soon decided he wasn't for me. It was not long after my friend had left for America that I decided to leave Hoovers. I cant remember why I left; in fact, I can't think of any logical reason why I would do so as the money was good and working with the girls on the line was enjoyable, but I suppose I must have had my reasons at the time.

My next job is working for Bush Radio in Power Rd Chiswick. This is a company that makes radios (obviously) and televisions. To get to work each morning I would get a 65 bus to Kew Bridge and then have about a ten minuet walk to Power Road. This time I am not working in the factory, but sit at a desk in a small office. I have tried hard to remember what sort of work I am doing but I can't; I am not even sure if there is a typewriter on my desk. It's funny sometimes how we can remember the places we have been, but not always the things we did there, and another time the things we do, but not where we did them - the mind is such a complex thing, or maybe its just so long ago.

While working at Bush Radio I made friends with two girls, one being single the other married. I have tried to reason which way it would be best to write about these friends as I cannot use their names, so I have decided to tell separately how each of them travelled with me on the road I was taking at that time.

Part 5.

FRIENDS

Even though I had had many jobs since leaving school, I still felt apprehensive when starting somewhere new, and this time was no different, but because everyone was helpful and always willing to show me the things I had to learn I soon settled in. I was not at this job long before I began to make new friends and the first one that becomes part of the road I am travelling sits at the desk next to mine. She is a very attractive girl with hair that is as black and shiny as a raven's, which she has grown to her shoulders, and across her forehead is a fringe which is cut very strait. When I first saw her she reminded me of pictures I had seen in books of Egyptian women, so would not have been surprised if she had told me that she bathed in milk and kept an asp in a basket under her desk. She said that she lived not far from Kew Bridge in a small terrace house with her mother. She was the youngest of her family, and as far as I can remember, had sisters who were all married. It was not many weeks after making friends with her that we decided to meet up after work. I did look forward to this, as since my other friend had left for America, life had become very mundane and I had wished that the Holiday Camp had not shut down for the winter months.

We arranged to meet on Kew Bridge, as this was not too far for her to walk from her house, and I could get a 65 bus, which would stop by the bridge. I remember we never quite knew what to do or were to go in those early days of our friendship, but that all changed when we discovered the ' Boat House,' but I will come to that later. I can see us now standing on the bridge trying to think what we could do with our evenings, and always ending with the decision of getting back on to a 65 bus that would take us to Richmond. Here we would walk around the town and then along by the river. I'm not sure if I remember the times that I had walked there before with the boy who was now thousands of miles away, but nothing stirs in my mind. Always, at the end of the evening, we ended up at a coffee bar and buy what we called Frothy Coffee, or the Italian-style coffee you would know as Cappuccino. This would be the highlight of the night. We would stand in line waiting for the coffee that was spooned from a large tin then put into a cup. Milk was added and then the cup was put under a machine where a spindle-like arm was dropped, and then a handle pulled down and a very loud noise which sounded like rushing steam was forced into the cup, and right before your eyes there was your coffee, all hot and milky with froth on the top which looked like the head on a pint of Guinness. When you put the cup to your mouth to drink, you would end up with a frothy moustache. How we would giggle at this. We took our coffee and sat at a table that was outside on a large balcony where other teenagers were either sitting or standing in groups. Again, I here you say, 'what is so special about coffee bars? We have them everywhere; we can sit outside any time and drink frothy coffee. But again you must remember that this is the 1950s, and coffee bars were new to us.

We had kept up this routine of going to Richmond for a time, when one day we decided that we would like to do something different but 'what,' we kept asking. Then, as we were looking over the bridge we noticed that there was a steady stream of people going into a public house that was built alongside the bridge called The Boat House. "How do you fancy going in there?" my friend said? Why not, I hear myself saying. We were not quite sure what we would find, but what a surprise, as the nearer we got to the entrance we began to hear the sound of music and of course that made my heart beat a little faster.

As we walked through the main doors, facing us were stairs, but the music was coming from the back of the pub, so we ignored these and headed straight for the sound. Then, pushing open the next set of doors, we found ourselves in the place that would become, for me, once again, one of the places in my life that I will always remember as being special.

I have tried to find a little bit of history for you on this building but have not been able to. So I can only describe what my memory tells me. I remember the bar, which was lit up by lights, on the right hand side as you walked through the doors, and about two yards in front of this were pillars spread around the room that seemed to hold up the ceiling above us. To the left of the doors, behind the pillars, were tables and chairs for people to sit. But in the middle of the room was what got my attention the most, for there was a small but long dance floor with a stage at the end, and on this sat a three piece band playing rock and roll. I had not danced since coming home from Clacton, so when I heard the music, I could not wait to get onto the dance floor. But now a thought came into my mind: could my friend dance? The subject of dancing had never come up.

We made our way to the bar to buy drinks, asking for two Shandies which cost us two shillings (about 10p), and decided not to sit at the tables, but to stay with the crowd that stood by the bar. When the band began to play my friend asked me 'can you dance?' I don't mind having a go, I say, and soon we were dancing, hardly ever pausing for breath. So, my friend could dance after all. As I am thinking and writing about this, I am imagining I am back there once again; I can see in my mind the lights over the bar. I'm hearing the beat of the music and feel the atmosphere, and I want to go back and be a teenager all over again.

Thursday, Friday and Saturday were the three evenings in the week that became the times I would look forward to the most. For these were the evenings I would meet my friend on the bridge and the next stop was the Boat House. There we would dance away the night. I remember I would spend ages trying to decide what to wear. Shall I put on a strait pencil slim skirt or perhaps a full skirt with yards of material? Shall I wear shoes with stiletto high heels or flat shoes with hardly any heel at all? Oh the decisions we have to make as teenagers! If I wore the full skirt I would wear a strait petticoat underneath so the tops of my stockings and my suspenders would not show when I twisted around. But in the end, I think it came down to mood I wanted to be in - was it sophisticated or girly?

Friday was still the day each week I collected my wages, so come the following Thursday, I would have no money left, but Dad always came to my rescue. Each Thursday I would ask to borrow two shillings (about 10p). That is what my night out would cost me. I would pay sixpence for my bus fare to the bridge, one shilling for a Shandy, and sixpence for my bus fare home. Then on Friday when I got my wages, I would repay Dad the two shillings. Then the following Thursday I would borrow all over again. Why didn't I put the two shillings away? I think as I am writing.

In the fifties the main mode of transport was either train or bus, and so, if you managed to find a boyfriend who had a motorbike or a car, this was a bonus you would try to hold on to for as long as possible. I met two boys around this time; both had motorbikes. The first one, who I can't remember how I met, had a big and powerful machine called a Vincent, and I loved it. I would never have to listen for the bell to ring when he came to call for me. He would pull up in front of the house and rev the throttle. I would grab my bag run down the stairs and next minute be sitting behind him with my arms wrapped tight around his waist while speeding off. The trouble was it was nearly always speeding to his home to just sit and talk to his parents. This boy did not go with the motor bike. So perhaps the only memories that stand out about him are the thrill of his bike and of another embarrassing moment. It was one day after work that he came to pick me up and I was wearing a flared skirt, which I had not tucked under myself very well when getting on the seat of the bike, and we had not gone very far when suddenly I felt this rip at my waist. Soon the bike was slowing down, and when we finally stopped, I looked and saw my skirt was entwined in the back wheel instead of round my waist. He was not happy. I had to run all the way home showing stockings and suspenders to everyone who passed. (Hope the seams in my stockings were straight!) We did not stay together for very long after that - he was too boring for me and I'm sure he never trusted me on his bike again.

I met the second boy one evening in the Boat House, and he stands out in my mind not because of his motorbike, which was not big and powerful, but small with a sidecar, but because he was such a good dancer, and I would spend most of the evening dancing with him. Occasionally we did meet at other times, but like the boys I had met previously, there was nothing more than friendship between us (but boy could this one dance!). Once again as I write, I ask myself where are they now? Where did there roads lead them? For the memories they give me and the smile they have brought to my face as I remember and write I hope the roads they have travelled have been good to them.

It had been several months since the friend I had met at the holiday camp had left for America, when one morning I received a letter from her to say that she was coming home. At first I thought that she must be missing her family, but as I read on she was telling me that not long after she had settled into her new job she found out that she was pregnant and that the boy she had met just before leaving was the father. I can't remember how I felt as I read this, perhaps sad because she had looked forward so much to starting a new life in a new country, or because being an unwed mother in the fifties would not prove an easy time for her. Many unmarried girls who became pregnant were sent away to homes to await the birth of their child, and then the baby would be put up for adoption. Most mothers had no say in this, as having children outside of marriage would bring disgrace on the family, and being rich or poor would bring the same disgrace. Sometimes, in order to keep the baby, the father would marry you, even though he might not want to. This meant that the baby would not be born out of wedlock and to give the baby a name, as the saying was then. These were known as shot gun weddings. But knowing her family as I did, I felt sure that she would be one of the lucky ones and get all the help that she needed in making the decisions that lay ahead of her.

I was still receiving letters from the boy I had nearly married, and even though I looked forward to reading them, I was not sure if I had the same feelings for him as before he went away. I had made a new life for myself and could not see marriage as part of it. His letters tell me that he is now in Borneo, which is the third largest island in the world, and that he is making friends with the Dayak people who live in the rain forests; of how there families all live together in huts, which are called 'long houses,' and of their women, who pierce the lobe of their ears then put weights on to them to stretch the lobe, reaching sometimes below there shoulders, and how they file there teeth into jagged edges so they are able to eat meat easier. He tells me also of all the different animals he has seen and describes the exotic birds that he sees every day, and by reading his letters, I know that the decision of joining the army was the best he could have made, and one he would never regret, so each time I receive a letter, I feel sure that he is going to tell me that he has decided to stay in the army for the twenty two years that he had signed for.

Even though I would write regularly to him, my letters were not as exciting or full of the wonders of the world as his were, but I did tell him of the places I had worked and the friends I had met, even dying my hair blond, but the one thing I always left out was the times I had spent with other boys. I did think on occasion perhaps I should end our relationship, but that would have meant sending him what was known as a 'Dear John letter.' This was a letter that was written by wives or girlfriends to servicemen when they had wanted to end their marriage or relationship, mainly because they had met someone else or did not want to wait for them to come home, but I could never make up my mind whether it was something I really wanted to do, and I knew deep down that I could not hurt him in this way, especially while he was so far from home. He often told me about the 'Dear John' letters that some of his fellow solders had received and how upset they were when they had read them, so this probably was the main reason I did not write one.

There were no complications in my life at this time; I was jogging along quite happy and content. I liked my job, I had made new friends, and my evenings were filled with the things I wanted to do. But then one Friday evening when I was standing by the doors at the Boat House I looked across at the bar and noticed that, staring back at me was a tall fair-haired boy. I turned away, pretending I had not noticed him, and then whispered to my friend saying 'don't make a big thing of it, but can you see the fair-haired boy standing by the bar, he's staring at me'. She gradually turned her head and looked. 'He's a bit of all right' she says, as she turns back to face me, but now he's not just staring, he's making his way across the floor towards me. 'He's coming this way' I whisper to her. The band has started playing a slow tune, and as I see him getting closer, I can feel my heart pounding in my chest. Is he going to ask me to dance? Or maybe he's just making his way to the door. Please don't let it be the door, I'm thinking. But now he's holding me close and I can feel myself shaking. 'What is wrong me? I'm thinking to myself. I've danced with lots of boys before, but I have never felt like this. He doesn't say much, and I'm glad, as I know that my voice will shake if I have to speak to him, but soon the music comes to an end and we both make our way back to our friends. Now the music changes tempo - its rock and roll, but he doesn't ask me for a dance this time. Instead, I dance with my friend, but all the time I can feel his eyes on me, so when the music finishes again I hope the next tune will be a slow one and he asks me to dance once more.

He did ask me to dance again, and so began a time in my life when feelings for another boy became as strong as the ones I had had for the boy that was now overseas. But he was so different - he was quiet and very shy, and sometimes I would find it hard to make conversation. I can't think of any places we went to other than the Boat House, and then he would only meet me inside. I remember once we arranged to meet at Ealing Broadway to go to the cinema; I waited but he never came, and then when I next saw him he did not even mention that he had let me down, and gave no reason why he had not turned up, but I never said anything either - again I ask myself why? Even though my feelings for him were still very strong, I gradually began to realise that no matter how I felt about him, he did not feel the same about me, or at least he never said that he did - but the funny thing was that at no time did he ever dance or spend time with anyone else during those three evenings a week, and because the weekend was involved in those days, I could not make up my mind if he was seeing anyone else besides me. I felt sure that if he was why did they not want to see him during the weekend? The only things he told me about himself were that he lived in Brentford, and that his job was that of a coalman. I don't think he told me anything about his family, as I am sure I would have remembered. So you see I knew very little about him. I am wondering as I write, because he was so shy with me maybe that was the reason that he found it difficult to make conversation and to let me know how he really felt. Or maybe for some reason it was my fault, and I was the one that kept him from telling me the things I wanted to hear. Why did I not ask more questions? Gradually, although we never said the words to stop seeing each other, he stopped coming to the Boat House so often. When he did turn up we would dance together, but there would be hardly any words spoken between us other than asking each other 'how are you?' and 'what have you been doing?'

As I write I am trying to remember how I felt at this time, as somewhere in the pit of my stomach I know that this boy was special to me, but I can't feel the pain that breaking up gives you. Maybe it's too long ago or maybe because too much has happened, or maybe because that was not the end of the story.

The town of Brentford comes into my life on several occasions, so I will give you just a little bit of history about this town. It is a very old town and predates the Roman occupation of Britain, and even predates the founding of London, and was first described as The Country Town of Middlesex in 1789. Between 1815 and 1817, John Quincy Adams, the sixth President of the United States of America lived here, and many other great names in history stayed and lived for a short while. Once again, I encourage taking time and seeking out the history of the places I have written about, as they will bring to life the history of the country you live in.

It was about this time that I received a letter telling me that my friend had arrived home from America and that she hoped I would visit soon. It was not long before I was knocking at her door, and once again there were laughter and tears. She looked well, but when she had left there was the look of a girl who was carefree, and now you saw the look of someone who was wondering what the future was going to be, but for a different reason. First she talked of how much she had enjoyed America and then how frightened she had been when she had found out that she was pregnant. The American family, she said, had been kind to her and had been disappointed that she would have to return home, and she too regretted that it had turned out this way. But said, in all her family's disappointment, they were giving her all the support that she needed and how arrangements were being made for her to marry, so giving me the impression that this was what she wanted. How glad I was that even though this time was difficult for her she was copping. She was a good friend and I wanted her to be happy. But there was a shock waiting around the corner. Her road was not going to be so easy after all.

Several weeks later she was married at a registry office, and when I went to visit her at her home not long afterwards, she told me that the father had not stayed with her but had gone back to live in his own home. Why would he do this? The reason to marry was just to give the baby a name. Whether she expected this to happen she never did say; maybe she hoped that he would change his mind once they were married. But when I looked at her, I saw the hurt that was coming from deep within, and my heart went out to her.

Now I'm at her door once again and being invited in where her family are all standing around with anxious faces. She has gone into labour I am told, and the midwife is with her; soon the cry of a baby tells us that the pain is all over, and by the sound of its lungs, it is telling us 'I want every one to know I am a boy and I have arrived!' I climb the stairs two at a time. I've been told I can meet the new arrival, and what a bundle of joy he is to my friend, as the look on her face now tells me that whatever the future has in store for her, her son will be the most important person in her life. Once again as I write, there are tears in my eyes.

Its a few weeks before I visit again, and now she is no longer talking about the things we did, but all about her young son. She telling me how much he weighs, how much he drinks and how long he sleeps and I think to myself 'is this the girl who not long ago was talking not about babies but of adventures in a foreign land?' Of course I never understood this feeling, as I had no children of my own, but how can you stop a mum talking about a new life which means so much to her?

It was on one of my evening visits to her that the father of her son turned up, and from the moment he stepped into the room the atmosphere changed. No longer was there joy on her face and a bounce in her voice; now all seemed sombre, and the atmosphere became very heavy. He said hallo to me and then they both left the room and climbed the stairs together to see the son who had changed both their lives, but when they soon came back down, he spoke as if living apart was the natural thing to do.

Soon it was time for me to leave, and because he had a car he offered to take me home, and all seemed fine until we stopped outside my house. I thanked him for the lift and was about to get out of the car when he said that he would like to take me out one evening, and then leaned forward as if he was about to kiss me! But I was quicker than he was, and told him in no fine words where to go - using such words that once again were not part of my everyday speech. As I lay in bed that night and thought of what was said, I knew that even though the future for my friend was not going to be easy, she would be far better off with out the complications she would probably have if she lived with this boy.

It's now nearly two years since I stood on the platform and watched the train leave; taking with it the life that I thought at that time had come to a standstill. Christmas will soon be here, and I have received a letter telling me that it won't be too long before I will be seeing the boy who leaned out of the train window not knowing what to say to me. Is it really two years? I say to myself. I think of the places I have been and of the friends I have made, and realise that these two years have not been so bad after all.

I am still going to the Boat House on Thursdays, Fridays and Saturdays, and still look forward to the excitement that I get when Thursday arrives. During those days I am still trying to make the decision of what to wear, not just for that night, but also for the whole weekend - always rushing home, eating my dinner as quickly as possible, waiting for the evening to begin; once again, the biggest decision of the day is 'what shall I wear' and by the time I have decided, its nearly time to catch the 65 bus to Kew Bridge to meet my friend. But hold on a minute - that is not just my friend waiting on the bridge for me, she has someone with her. It's her mother. Why is she waiting with her daughter, I wonder. I was soon to find out, for the next minuet she is telling me that she does not want her daughter staying out till all hours of the morning, and that I was a bad influence on her. I stood there not knowing what to say, for I could not understand why she should say this - I was never out till all hours of the morning (more's the pity). What is your mum on about?

I ask my friend as soon as her mother leaves, and its then she tells me that she has been seeing a boy on the nights we don't go out and spending time with him, and because she did not want her mother to know, had said she was with me. Now I knew why her mother had never made me feel welcome when I had visited her home! Although I was not happy that her mother felt that I was to blame for her daughter's late nights, and was a little disappointed that my friend had not owned up even when her mother was blaming me, because she was my friend and she apologised it was soon forgotten just a few days later she's telling me that she is getting married. Even though this seems the end of the road I was travelling with this friend, that is not so, and I will bring her in to my story later.

Now I must tell you about the other friend I made while working at Bush Radio. As I said earlier, she was married even though she was not much older than me. I remember her husband was quite a bit older than she was and they lived in a terrace house in Acton, West London, that was soon to be pulled down to make way for new council flats, and she was going to be offered one of these. In the 1950s it was the government's idea to pull down rows of housing that was looked on a slum to make way for very high blocks of flats, and it was one of these that the council was going to offer her. My memory of her is that she was a very gentle person and in whose company I was always happy to be. Because she was married, our friendship was not one of going out dancing, but I would be invited to her home where we would have girly conversations with lots of giggling. I remember that when I visited her she would always insist on not just giving me cups of tea, but making me stay for supper, and it was nearly always mushroom omelette with chips and peas. Because she lived quite far away from me, I would have to get the train to Acton and still have quite a walk to her house. Often during the dark nights her husband would walk me back to the train station to make sure I got there safely. You can see what a nice couple they were, and the impression I got from this friend was that she was very happy in her married life, and so was very surprised at the road she took when, in her future, she reached a cross roads. But that too I will tell you about later.

The next place I see myself working is as an usherette and cashier in the Walpole Cinema in Bond Street. I gave you a little history on this cinema earlier, and of course at that time I never thought I would ever work there. Once again, I cannot remember why I left my previous job at Bush Radio. I have happy memories of working there, so why I left I am not sure. I sometimes think as I look back that I never stayed long at any of my places of employment, because they were jobs that I really did not want to do, and even though I was happy for awhile, I soon got bored and needed to move on. The only place I know I would have stayed at was the holiday camp, not because of cleaning chalets, but because of the life that it gave me and the faces that changed each week. Maybe it all started when leaving school - I was not allowed to choose what job I wanted. I am trying to find a reason, but is there one?

Christmas has been and gone, and a new year is just days away. Now all I have on my mind is the boy who will soon be home from Singapore. In what ways will he have changed I wonder. How will he feel about me? But hold on now, I suddenly think - how will I feel about him? Will I be glad that I did not send him a 'Dear John' letter? Soon I will know the answer to these questions but as I think about them, I wonder what the new road I am about to take has in store for me.

Part 6.

HOME COMING

The month is January, the day is Saturday, the weather is cold and Mum is in bed with the flu. I am standing at the side of her bed while she is writing a shopping list, and as I look out the window - crossing the road, heading for my house, is the boy that I have been waiting two years for. I did not have to look twice to make sure it was him; I would know his walk anywhere. It's **him**, he's **here,** I say to Mum, who has been nearly as excited about his coming home as I have. My heart begins to beat that little bit faster, and I can feel butterflies in my tummy. But I don't run down the stairs, instead I wait for the doorbell to ring. "Go and answer the door Mum" says, but I can't move - it's as if I'm stuck to the floor. Don't keep him waiting, answer the door! She says. Now I'm running down the stairs and I open the door. He's standing there with a big grin on his face and now I'm in his arms and he's kissing me; I can't breathe I say, but I don't really want him to let me go. Soon he is climbing the stairs two at a time, pulling me behind him. Mum is in the front room I say, she's in bed with the flu, and Dads in the kitchen. He's giving Mum a hug and Dad is shaking his hand. "You look well boy" Dad says, how's it been then? Soon we are all sitting around Mum, drinking tea and listening to some of his tales. I was just going to do some shopping I say; come on we'll go together he says. Again as I write I ask myself did we really, after not seeing each other for two years, spend those first hours going to the shops. What peculiar mortals we are.

When did you get home I asked. "I arrived in England yesterday" he says, but had to go straight to the barracks, then caught a train early this morning. "I bet your Mum was happy to see you" I say. Yes she was he says - SHE WANTS ME TO GO TO THE CLUB TONIGHT.

Suddenly I'm not walking towards Ealing Broadway, as my memory and imagination are taking me back two years to those hours that I spent at the club before he went away, and I say to myself 'do I want to go down that road again?' and the answer is no. Does your Mother know you have come to see me I ask him, 'no he say's' and that tells me that she is not going to be too pleased when she sees me. "You will come to the club?" he asks, and I reluctantly say yes, trying not to sound disappointed. But how can I spoil his first night home; I do understand that he must be with his parents, as they have been without their son for two years.

It's not long before I am sitting upstairs on a 607 bus feeling very apprehensive about meeting his Mum and Dad again. I am remembering the letter that his Mum sent to him, saying that I was seeing other boys, so that tells me that being in her company may be strained. But the boy sitting at the side of me does not show that he is at all concerned, so perhaps I am worrying over nothing.

Now we are walking through the doors and into the lounge at the club and soon all eyes turn towards us. Everyone smiles, even his Mother, but her smile soon disappears when she sees me. She says 'hallo' but I know by her tone and the look on her face that she is not happy that I am there, and that tells me I should not have agreed to come. My attention is quickly drawn elsewhere, as soon we are being made a fuss off by the rest of the people there. How glad they were to see us they said, and especially how pleased they were to see the boy that many had known as a child, he'd left home as a boy but now returned as a man. Questions were now being put to him 'where did you go? What did you do there? Did you want to come home? Are you going back?' Soon it was as if he had never been away, and his beaming smile tells me that he is glad to be home and amongst the people he has known all his life.

I can't remember how many days it was before he had to return to the barracks, and I can't remember what it was like being with him during those first days we were together. I only know that he told me that he had decided not to stay in the army for the full amount of time, so it was only going to be a matter of weeks before he would be demobbed. I know that I was really pleased to hear this, but did wonder what the road ahead would hold for us both, and also knew that it was not going to be an easy ride for us as once he was demobbed, first he would have to get used to being out of the army; second, I was not sure if we could take up our relationship where we left off, as we were both different people now; and third I knew that his Mother was not happy about him being with me.

I soon introduced him to the Boat House, but after going a couple of times he began to make excuses for not wanting to go. I even took him to meet my friends who lived in Acton, but this too he seemed reluctant to do. I wonder if he is missing the army, and even suggest that he signs on again, but he says no, he is glad to be home with me. We go to the club occasionally, but the atmosphere with his Mother has become so strained it's my turn to make excuses, and I begin to realise that it will never be any different between his Mother and me and cannot understand why she feels the way she does. Perhaps I should have asked her.

It was not long after he was demobbed that he began working at St. Bernard's Mental Hospital, which is the hospital just outside the town of Southall that I told you about earlier, and because he had finished his apprenticeship in the army, he was now able to get a job as a qualified plumber and heating engineer. He used to tell me how much he enjoyed working there and said how well he got on with the patients, and because he was now settled in a job, he said that we should think about getting married. It was not long after he came home that he asked me to start wearing the engagement ring that he had given to me before he went away, so I knew that marriage was on his mind, and because of this, it was no surprise that he wanted to set a date for a wedding. But things were not going right between us

- how could he not see that? I began to wonder: was he just closing his mind to the strained atmosphere between his Mother and me? Or maybe he just felt obligated. We did talk about it but he just brushed it off. Could he not see how unhappy I was beginning to be? I no longer ran to open the door when he rang the bell and now there were long silences between us; we no longer seemed to have anything in common and instead were drifting apart. Mum must have noticed that there was something wrong, as she kept asking me if everything was alright. I began to remember the words my Dad had said just before this boy had gone away 'feelings for each other could change in two years, but the time separated would give us both a chance to be sure of what we wanted'.

How right he was. How could I think of marrying? But how was I going to tell him it was all over? I came to the conclusion that there would never be an easy way, but I still could not face him, knowing that when the time came to say those words I would look at his face and would change my mind. So I took the coward's way out as a plan began to form in my mind. I decided to write him a letter and then get the train to Clacton. As the holiday season had begun, the holiday camp would come to my rescue. I would go away hoping that, as before, I could start a new road in my life. I knew that going away this time would be different for Mum and Dad and felt sure that they would understand my reasons for doing this. The next task was to write the letter. I don't remember what I wrote; I only remember that I put the letter in the envelope and at that moment had no regrets, and the morning I left for the holiday camp I posted it.

What was I thinking on that train journey as each mile was taking me further away from the life I thought had been mapped out for me? Probably asking myself, once again, have I done the right thing? Why is it when you think you are going down one road you suddenly end up going down another? What did I say at the beginning of my story 'Life, what a funny word - what does it mean?'

Arriving at the camp was so different this time I did not feel like the new girl that every one was staring at. I was back on the chalet line as a Chalet Maid, and within a couple of days I had settled back into the routine as if I had never been away. The room I had been given was much better than the one I had previously, which made it all the easier to settle in. But even though every thing at the camp was going well for me, I still had an awful feeling in the pit of my stomach. Was it there because I had made a hasty decision again? Had I taken a road which once again I would regret? I kept thinking of the letter I had sent, wondering how it had been received. Maybe I should have been less of a coward and faced him. But it was too late now, and the only one who I knew would be pleased at this outcome would be his Mother.

It was about two weeks later, while I was busy on my chalet line that a supervisor came and said that there was someone waiting for me in reception. Immediately I knew who that someone was. As I made my way across the camp, my mind began to race, going over all the reasons why he had come. When I saw him I am sure my heart skipped a beat, and I knew in that moment that I should never have written the letter, but instead had the courage to face him. He said that he had come to talk and to try to straighten out the problems that had arisen between us, but instead of telling him I was glad to see him, all I said was 'I'm sorry but I can't talk now, as I am still working.' So he said he would look around the camp and meet me at reception when I finished work.

As I walk back to my chalet line my mind is in turmoil, as one second I am glad he is here, but in the next, I wish he had never come. I already know all the things he is going to say to me but what are my answers going to be? The only thing I was sure of was that he must care for me or he would not have wasted his weekend to come and find me. For the rest of the afternoon this was all I could think about.

I met him as soon as I finished work and we spent the next couple of hours talking over all the problems there were between us, till finally he persuaded me to give up my job at the camp and return home. Did I do the right thing? I don't know. I only knew that when I went to the personnel office to tell them I was leaving, there was still something inside me that wished I had said no. But what really made me doubt my decision was when we finally reached home, he said to Mum and Dad: see I told you I would bring her home! (With a sound of conquest in his voice).

The first thing I had to do on coming home was to look for employment, and so found myself a job working at the Dome garage on the Great West Road. Again I cannot remember much about this job, only that I worked in a small office, and the journey to work was easy - all I had to do was catch a 65 bus at the top of my road to the Great West Road; providing I did not have to wait too long for the bus, it would only take minutes.

Now a different road was being marked out for me, as plans for a wedding were being talked about. Mum had kept several of the items that I had saved for my bottom draw the first time I had become engaged, but these were not nearly enough to set up a home with. So began the endless task of trying to think of the items I would need to start my married life. I remember on one occasion when I went to see my Nan, she took me to West Ealing and bought a kitchen table and four chairs as a present. In my mind I can still see these so clearly - they were a very bright yellow with black spots, which looked like smudges all over them. The table had a Formica top; the backs and seats of the chairs were padded, and the legs were very thin and spindly. Funny really when I look back, because we still had nowhere to live and at the time I was not sure if I would have anywhere to put them. But I love my Nan for doing that.

So began the task of house hunting, or should I say 'room' hunting, which is very different. There was no way that we were able to buy a house as neither of us were earning the money to put a deposit down and then pay off a mortgage, so room hunting it was. We began to look on notice boards and in the local paper to see if we could find anywhere suitable, but even this became a much bigger task than I expected. We looked at so many. There were ones that were so small you could just about squeeze between the wall and the bed; others that smelt of damp and some where the landlord did not want couples. But the biggest problem was his Mother, as she had continued to say she did not want her son to marry me. I remember one evening we had met each other straight from work and I had walked with him to his house; as we got to his front door his Mother was sitting in the window (as she normally did) and saw us coming, and as soon as we entered the living room she said to me "You go to work with him now do you?" I thought she was just making a joke, so I began to laugh, but she was not joking as in her next breath she was shouting at us both telling us that there was no way she was going to come to the wedding, he just said "You must do what you want," and with that, we went out of the front door.

I can't remember how the rest of that evening went, but my memory tells me that it could not have been good, but soon our spirits were lifted as we eventually found a little room at the top of a house in West Ealing. The room was not very big but was very clean and had in it a bed, a basin, a small cooker with two rings and a small oven, chest of draws and a small cupboard built into the wall. Oh, and it had a table and two chairs, which I asked the landlord if he did not mind could I bring my own, to which he agreed. To heat the room there was a small gas fire (there is a little story about the gas fire which I will tell you about later), and the rent for this room was two pounds ten shillings per week. When we got married I was earning about five pounds per week, so between us, it was about 16 before our stoppages.

Soon the day drew near for the marriage to take place. Mum had asked Nan if we could have a small reception at her house, to which she agreed, and all aunts and uncles were invited. I had bought my dress and the wedding was booked at Ealing Registry Office. His brothers and their families were happy for us and were looking forward to coming to the wedding, but we still did not know if his Mum and Dad would change their minds and turn up.

It was the Friday night before the big day and everyone was rushing around doing all the things you have to do. I don't know what must have been going on in my mind, but suddenly I felt that I just needed to escape. While Mum was over at Nan's, I left a note on the mantelpiece saying I was going to see my friend. I knew that Mum would not be happy about this as she rightly expected me to stay and help with all the preparations, but at that moment I just had to go. As I made my way to my friend's house I must have been thinking 'why on earth I am sitting on a bus going to visit a friend when I should be helping to arrange my own wedding?' My friend from Kew had not yet married, so I was hoping that she would be home when I called as she was not expecting me. The look of surprise on her face when she answered the door said "What are you doing here? But all she said was 'wait there,' then she ran and got her coat, shouted to her Mum that she was going out, then shutting the door behind her she grabbed my arm as we started walking. Aren't you supposed to be at home she says? Changed your mind have you? No, just needed to get away for a while I say. Not easy getting married she says. I too have been wondering what married life for me is going to be like. I too feel like running away some times. But her very next question is 'do you want to go to the Boat House?' How could I resist that invitation? So instead of getting the bus home, I found myself standing at the bar ordering two shandies. Whether I felt guilty about being there I do not remember, but what I do know is that as I looked around staring at me is the boy I had previously met and had liked. It was not long before he came over and asked me to dance. 'How have you been,' he asks. 'OK' I say. What have you been doing? He asks again. Oh this and that I say, making no mention that I am getting married the following day.

Soon the music finishes and I am back with my friend. Did you tell him you are getting married? No, I say, and she doesn't say a word.

That night he took me home but I still did not tell him I was getting married. Why, I ask myself, but I can not give you an answer, because I just do not know.

When I climbed the stairs to our flat all was quiet. As I pushed open the door to the kitchen, there were Mum and Dad waiting for me. I thought at first they were going to be angry that I had not stayed and helped them prepare for the following day, but all they said was that everything was ready at Nan's, and then asked if I was OK. But the look on Dad's face was asking more than this, so the next question was: are you sure you want to go through with this? I said yes.

Again, as I look back, I chose to take a road that many other people have taken with no idea where this road is going. Perhaps if we knew what was ahead we would choose a different route, perhaps change our minds and go a different way. But how are we to know? What makes any of us that special person who knows the outcome of our future?

Part 7

WALL FLOWER
(FAITHFUL IN MISFORTUNE)

"You make your bed, you lay on it" is a very well known and used saying. Whether this saying is said to young people today I'm not sure, but when I was a teenager, this phrase was used constantly among the older generation. So I began to make my bed in 1958 with the boy I had met in a cinema as a very young girl, and who had asked her friend not to move seats as I did not want him to sit next to me. As I arrived at the registry office, I noticed family and friends were standing on the pavement waiting for my arrival, and among them were his mother and father. So, they had decided to come after all. But there was no time to dwell on this, as the next minute the door of the car was opened and I was grabbed by the hand, being pulled up the steps that led to the room where the marriage would take place.

If I am honest, I have to say that there are not many things I remember about that day; I only know I was married and have a signed marriage certificate and a wedding photo that proves it. But I do remember slipping away with one of my aunts, the one who would plait her hair so fast as I would sit and watch as a child. She was married now to a boy that was in the Air Force, and seemed happy in her new life. She came with me to the room that was to be my home in West Ealing. We took with us some of the wedding presents and she helped me make the bed with the sheets and blankets that I had been given (no Continental quilts then). We made the room look as cosy as we could, with flowers in a vase and a pretty cloth on the table, and before I shut the door to go back to my reception, I took one last look at the room and felt that the new road I was about to take was going to be a happy one.

We had made arrangements to go on honeymoon, not straight away, but a fortnight later, to Ramsgate - why Ramsgate you might ask, and why a fortnight after the wedding? The only reason I can think of, as such a long time has past, is that Ramsgate was the place that I was taken to with Mum and Dad on holiday after the war had finished and people started having family holidays once again. Why a fortnight later? After spending what we had on the wedding and rent for the room, we had very little money left for our honeymoon, so we postponed it for two weeks, and how do I know we had little money is because I went to a pawn shop in West Ealing and pawned my engagement ring, putting the money I was given towards our holiday.

Pawn shops were places you would go to get a quick loan with out any fuss. They would look at the item you took in, and then tell you how much they would lend you on the item. If you agreed to this they would give you the money plus a ticket which you would keep. You had a certain amount of time in which to collect the item, paying back the money you had borrowed plus a small amount of interest. People would pawn no end of different items such as sheets, blankets and men's suits - in fact any item you can think of, and if they were not collected by the date on the ticket the pawn broker would keep them and then sell them. You could always recognise the pawn brokers by the symbol of three large gold balls that hung from outside the shop. Did I really start my married life this way? I am thinking as I write. Perhaps this should have given me some clue as to what lay ahead? I did redeem my engagement ring, but that was not the last time I paid a visit to the pawn broker.

We now found ourselves in Ramsgate. Ramsgate is an old fishing town with white cliffs and a large harbour, and it was from here in 1940 during the Second World War that four thousand two hundred fishing boats sailed to Dunkirk, France to rescue serving men from the beaches. But when we arrived in Ramsgate and went to our boarding house we were told that the room that we had booked was now unavailable, as we had cancelled and then rebooked, and because they were full for the week we had wanted. They managed to get us into another boarding house where we would sleep each night, but for breakfast we would have to walk back down the hill to theirs. I remember that the room we were eventually given was in a very large house that stood on top of a hill, with a staircase that was very wide, and when we were shown to our room, facing us was a very large four-poster bed. I remember we were asked if we would like a pot of tea in the mornings, but as we were not sure if we would have to pay extra for this and because we had so little money, we said no. Again, there is not a lot I remember about our holiday - just two occasions stand out in my memory. On the first night after coming home from walking around the town, we had not been in our room long when we heard laughing coming from the landing outside, and the next minute two people had opened our door and were standing in our room, but the look on their faces when they realised they had come into the wrong room by mistake was precious and something we often laughed about. Also a couple who we met on the train journey who had married that day spent the whole journey telling us about their wedding. We spent some time with them during the week, and even went to visit them one Christmas at their home, but after a while we lost contact with them and have never seen or heard from them again. I hope the road they travelled was good.

As soon as we returned home I settled in to the routine of married life. I would get up each day, go to work and now think not about going out to meet my friends, but 'what are we going to have for dinner.' I did the washing and ironing and kept our little room spick and span. I bought flowers that brought sunshine to the room, and of an evening we played cards for match sticks and listened to the wireless that had been given to us by my Dad. We used his wages to live on and mine we put away and saved. On Sundays we were invited to dinner by my Mum and Dad and, sometimes my aunt would come and visit us whenever her husband was home on leave from the Air Force. It was a different life than I had been used to as a single person, but I was happy and felt that I was adapting to not just thinking about myself, but the other person in my life.

Everything was about to change, as I found myself going down another road - one I did not expect so soon. I was pregnant. I began to be very sick, not just in the mornings, but on and off all day, so that in the end I had to give up my job. But our main concern at that moment was how the landlord would react to the news of my being pregnant, as there was no mention of children when we had moved in, and rented rooms normally came with the clause 'No Children.' Also, there was not a lot of government protection for people in furnished rented accommodation then, so you were normally given just a week's notice to quit. We did not tell the landlord straight away, and began to look for other accommodation just in case he said we could not stay. Each day I would search the notice boards, hoping that I would find someone willing to let with children, and each evening when he came home from work I would have to tell him that I had not found anything. Eventually the time came when we had no choice but to tell the landlord, and when we did all he said was 'sorry but you can't stay.' Living in that little room was no longer the haven it had been for me. Each morning as I opened my eyes I worried about what the day would bring. We were getting nowhere as far as finding somewhere else to live. What was I going to do when the baby arrived? If only we could stay in this room, I kept thinking to myself. The room is small, but at least we would have a roof over our heads.

Soon it is autumn, and as the weather is getting colder, the feeling of apprehension is growing more and more each day. Despite all the hours of searching in West Ealing, as well as Ealing Broadway and Hanwell, we still have been unable to find any place to rent, and because I have to spend more time at home and the days are getting colder, heating the room becomes more expensive. If you remember, I told you about the gas fire in our room. It was fed by putting money into a meter that would be emptied by the landlord every few weeks, and now that I was home so much, all I seemed to do was feed it, and as there was only one wage coming in, money was becoming very tight. I decided to buy a paraffin oil heater which, for a gallon of oil, would cost two shillings. This was not only cheaper than running the gas fire, but the oil would also last longer. I did know that the landlord would not be too happy about this, as the money from the meter went towards his gas bill for the whole house, but using the oil heater was the difference between affording to keep warm or being cold. Every Monday evening the landlord knocked on our door for the rent, and this particular evening was the time he chose to empty the meter as well. At first he never noticed the oil fire and just went straight to empty the meter. When he tipped the money into his hands and realised that there was hardly anything there, he turned and looked towards the fireplace and saw not his gas fire on, but our oil heater, and his next words told us he was not happy.

At last we found two rooms, again at the top of a house in West Ealing. The two rooms consisted of a bed-sitting room in the front of the house, which I cannot describe because I can not remember what it looked like, and a kitchen that was at the back of the house. All I remember about it is the sink and the table and chairs that my Nan had bought for me that we took with us. When we first moved in we thought how lucky we were to have found this place as the couple knew I was pregnant, so that would not be a problem, and because they had a young baby themselves, they would understand when a baby cried. They said if there was anything we needed we just had to ask, so because of there friendliness toward us we thought we had at last found a place we could settle. Everything was fine for a while, but then for some reason the wife's attitude changed, and I could not understand why. We were good tenants, we paid our rent on time, we never had the wireless too loud, we were always polite to them; in fact we only spent a few minuets with them when paying the rent, so why things changed I had no idea.

It all started not long before my baby was due. I was just going out the front door when she called me and said that she did not want me to have a large pram in the passage, so too make sure I bought a small one. That was the start of all sorts of do's and don'ts. It seemed as though each time I got to the front door, she would appear from her room and make a comment. It got so bad that I used to creep down the stairs, hoping I could be out the front door before she realised I was there. Once again, I knew that it would not be long before we would be looking for another place to live, as there was no way we could stay there. But the decision to leave was not left to us, as the next time he went down to pay the rent they said they felt they could not cope with having another baby in the house and would like us to leave by the end of the week. This was a shock. We thought they would at least give us more time, as they must know how hard it would be to find someone that would let with children. How could we find another place to live in five days? I was nine months pregnant and soon to be without a home again. What are we going to do, I ask him?

Now we were in deep trouble - where can we find a place to live at such short notice? The following day, as soon as he had left for work, I got dressed and left to search every notice board I could find. Each day was the same routine - I would dress, have breakfast, then leave, hoping that this was the day I would be lucky, but there were no new cards pinned to the notice boards, there were still plenty of rooms to let but all said "no children." It was now Friday, and still I had found nothing. When he came home and I had told him once again that I had still not be able to find any thing, he became very quiet, and the next words he said were "our only way out is to ask my Mum and Dad if we can stay with them, as they have a spare bedroom." My heart sank. How can I describe to you the feeling that came over me? Never in a million years would I have guessed that I would end up having to live with his parents, and I expect they felt the same way. How will your Mum feel about having me in the house, I say? But where else can we go? He says. So that night while I stayed in and rested, he went to see his Mum and Dad. I'm sure it was not easy for him to ask them, but it was no fault of his that we were in this situation - a situation that thousands of couples besides ourselves found themselves in every day. So began a period of living with his parents, of which I will be forever grateful but it did not go to plan as we thought it would. When he arrived home from seeing his parents, he said that they had agreed that we could stay there, but they would first have to get permission from the Council, and said that I could stay at their house at the weekend, but then I must go home to my mum and dad during the week until the permission came through, and as the Council only met once a month, they weren't sure when that would be. Now I had to face Mum and Dad. The look on their faces when I told them said that they were not at all happy. I remember that as I was telling them I began to cry, and wished I would wake up soon and find out that it had all been a bad dream.

We packed up all our belongings and moved some of our things to his parent's house and stayed there for the weekend. Monday morning after he left for work his mum asked me what I was going to do. I said I would stay till he finished work that evening and then he would take me home to my parent's house. "You can't do that" she said; the rent woman comes today, and I don't want her to see you here. So I quickly got dressed and said I would go and look around the town, but the one thing I forgot to do was to ask her what time the rent woman called. Now it wasn't just looking around the shops for a couple of hours, but staying out all day just walking, waiting for time to pass. As the afternoon came, it started to pour with rain, so I walked to the local park and sat in the shelter for a while before I made my way back to the shops and walked around again.

I could not wait for that day to come to an end, and when I had told him about the sort of day I had had he was not pleased, and said the rent woman comes early in the morning, you could have come home much sooner. But how was I to know? I had never lived at his house; I certainly never knew when the rent was collected. All I wanted to do now was to go to my bed and curl up, but I still had a long bus ride and a long walk home to face; would this day ever come to an end? What was I thinking at that time? If I was thinking then what I am thinking now, I cannot believe that this situation had arisen so early in my marriage. I would soon be on my third home and we had not been married very long. What must have been going through my mind as I lay in bed that night? I could only be thinking and wondering 'where is this road that I am travelling taking me?' and as I remember, a cold shiver is coming over me.

It was only a few days after moving back home that during the night I went into labour. The instructions that had been given to me by my doctor were to call the midwife, who would then tell me what hospital I would be going to, but when she came she said that the baby was nearly ready to be born, and asked Mum if I could have it at home, but Mum said no, so the next minute I'm in the back of an ambulance being taken to West Middlesex Hospital in Isleworth. This hospital was built in 1894. It was originally built as an infirmary for the New Brentford Workhouse, then over the years became a community hospital. Extra buildings have been added as the population has grown, so it now covers a vast area.

What am I now going to do with this small bundle of joy of 6 pounds, 14 ounces that I hold in my arms? As tiny as he is, he is round and chubby, and as I hold him close and feel the warmth of him the joy that I feel can never be explained. He is not like the doll that I had as a child who Dad had stuck long silver flaxen onto its head to make it look more real, and that I had loved even though its hair fell out when I combed it. This feeling was so different and I knew it would last me all my life. I stayed in hospital for five days after having him, as there was no going home the same day after your baby was born then, and it was only your husband or a close relative that was allowed to come visit you. Also, there was no picking the baby up, as it was kept in a nursery, and not in a cot at the side of your bed, so unless it cried for a period of time, it was only at feeding times you would have it with you.

At last it was time to leave hospital and take my baby, home but where were we going to go? I had no home. Each day that he had come to see me I had asked him if his parents had received the letter from the council, and he had said no. My mum had not said that I could take the baby there, and I knew that his mum was not happy for me to stay at his house till she received permission, so as I packed up all the items I had taken to the hospital, and dressed my little bundle of joy, all I could think about was where were we going to go. Soon he turned up to take me home, and as he walked towards my bed I was looking to see if there was a look on his face that would tell me that everything was going to be alright, but he just picked up my bag, and as we walked to the entrance of the hospital I asked him "where are we going?" We are going to stay at my brothers until the letter comes from the council, he says. At least we will be together, were his next words. He was right - we would be together, but again I will be living with people that I do not really know. Even though they had always been nice to me, living with them would be different, and it wasn't just us that would be in their house - I would be bringing a baby as well. He must have seen a look on my face that showed utter despair, as his next words were 'its not going to be long before the Council should meet,' but even though I was grateful for the help I was being given, I could not bring myself to smile and again I am thinking 'is it always going to be like this?' As we reach the entrance of the hospital there is my Dad waiting for us in his shiny new car, and as I get into the car I see the look on Dad's face as he turns to me; he doesn't say a word, but I know what he is thinking.

As you may have noticed, it is not a motorbike that Dad is driving now, but a car. It is a Ford Prefect family car, which has now become his pride and joy. I can't remember exactly when he bought it or why he swapped it for the motorbike, but I do know that whenever he could, he would be washing and polishing it till it shone and woe betide anyone who put their dirty fingers on it. As I am writing this I can see him now with his sleeves rolled up, a rag in his hand, rubbing the polish into the bonnet, going round and round, and I can also see the cup of tea that is on the pavement beside him, which nearly always ended up forgotten or, when remembered, was too cold too drink. This car was one of several he had over the years, and each one would get the same loving treatment. But the story about the last one that he owned is the one that stands out in my memory - this is a story that will come later.

We went straight to his brother's on leaving the hospital, and when I arrived, most of the baby items and clothes for me had already been taken there, but once again, I felt so out of place. This was not my home, and even though his brother and sister-in-law did their best to make me feel welcome, I never felt any better. They had set aside one of their bedrooms for us, but I can't tell you anything about this room, or the house, because it has gone completely from my memory. I can't even tell you how long we stayed with them; my only memory is that they tried hard to make our stay as comfortable as possible, and was very kind.

Eventually his mother received a letter from the Council giving permission for us to move in with them, but again we were going somewhere where I did not want to be. As you read this I do not want you to get the impression that I was not grateful to them for giving a home to a virtual stranger plus a new baby. I know it could not have been easy for them either, but for me it was not what I had dreamed of. I had always been brought up to believe that marriage was about having a home of your own. There had been nothing in my dream that had prepared me for what I had experienced so far in my marriage.

When we finally moved into their home we were given one of the front bedrooms, which, with their permission, we made into a bed-sitting room. We thought by doing this it would give us and them privacy. We bought two Lloyd loom chairs and a settee which at night could be made into a bed, and because the Council had now installed electricity, we even managed to buy a small television, which was now becoming popular with most households. Each day I tried my best to keep to some sort of routine by first seeing to my baby's needs, then doing the washing and any ironing which, seemed never ending since having him. If the weather was fine to put him in his pram, we would walk to town. I would look forward to five thirty p.m., for this was the time that he would be home from work, and it was the time that I felt more relaxed by him being there. Most weekends we would visit Mum and Dad, then Mum and I would walk to West Ealing, spending time looking around the shops, sometimes leaving the baby with him, but when I did this, all I had on my mind was the baby. I need never to have worried, as he was always fine with his Dad, who loved him and used to say 'I don't know what you're worried about.'

It must have been about seven months that we stayed with his parents, still always looking for a home of our own and, considering the situation was something that neither of us had expected, the time spent with them had turned out very well; there were never any bad feelings, and they loved their grandson very much.

During this time my sister had met a boy and had married, and as they too were looking for somewhere to live, we all agreed with the idea that if we could find a house to share we would each pay half the rent. I cannot remember the reason that we felt we would be better off leaving his parent's to go down this new road. As I write and think now, it was not the brightest move we should have made, but I began to feel excitement at the idea that I would soon start going down another road, one that would take me on a journey where at last I could settle and make a home for him and **my son**. Again I began to dream of the ideal family, with all that went with it.

I saw myself waiting for the end of each day when he would see me waiting for him at the door when he arrived home from work, with my baby in my arms greeting him, and then sharing with him all the wonderful things I had done during the day. I could almost hear birds singing and cooing over my head. The dream was wonderful - at last everything would turn out right. But the dream turned into a nightmare. If only I had known how things would turn out, I would never have even put my toe to the ground to take that step. I thought that living with his parents was difficult for me, but nothing could have prepared me for what lay ahead as I started on the next road on the map.

Sometimes there are obstacles in our way, but because of wanting to reach out for some things, we think are better; we don't, or choose not to see them, and this was a road which once again was going to take me in another direction; it would be a road of hard work and disappointments, sometimes giving me feelings of utter despair, and it was the beginning of a new road that would go on for many years with lots of turns and hills to climb.

It was not long before we managed to find a house that was big enough for both families. We agreed that the rent, gas and electric bills would first be halved and then we would pay a little extra as we had the baby, which would reduce their contribution. The house we found was in Perivale, which again, is in the west of London. It was a lovely house in a quiet suburban street with two nice size rooms downstairs, plus a scullery which (now called kitchens), and three bedrooms and a bathroom upstairs, plus a back garden. The house was let to us unfurnished and, as there was no cooker in the kitchen, the first priority was the purchase of one of these, which my sister and her husband said they would buy. Also in the kitchen was a china sink which they decided to replace with a new sink unit. We each had a room downstairs as our sitting room, and the same upstairs for our bedroom, and it was agreed that the baby would have the small box room as his bedroom, where we put his cot and later, a small wardrobe which was given by them for the baby. I cannot remember how we furnished the rooms; I know we took with us the bed settee and the two chairs plus the television we had bought while living with his mother, but have no memory of anything else.

So began a period of what seemed at first the ideal solution to our housing problem, and as I was the only one not going out to work, being in the house on my own during the day with just the baby were times I really enjoyed. I did all the things I had dreamed about: looking after the house, taking my baby out in his pram, and having the tea on the table at the end of the day and greeting him with the words 'how has your day been?' Soon there was another surprise. I found myself once again pregnant, but we were happy about this, as we felt we were settled for a while; so all my dreams were coming true - or so I thought.

Since we had moved to Perivale he had changed his job, and was now working at the Hoover Factory where I had previously worked. It was not using his trade as a plumber, but on an assembly line. I can't remember why he gave up plumbing to do this, but once again there must have been a reason. Soon dark clouds began to gather, with no silver lining, for the one thing we had all forgotten was that my sister and her husband were not used to living with a baby in the house, and because of this they did not seem to understand that partying and playing loud music till all hours most weekends and some times during the week was not something you could do with a baby in the house. Because of this, the atmosphere now started to become strained between us. I remember at one of their parties, lots of food had been bought and the centre piece for the table was a pig's head, which at the time was something that a lot of people would use. It was not for eating but just for show, and when the party was over it was taken out and put in a bag by the dustbin waiting for the dustman to collect. But while waiting for the collection a fly must have found its way inside the bag, for when a few days later we looked outside, there, crawling everywhere were what seemed like hundreds of maggots. It was one of the worst sites I had ever seen and have never used or smelt so much disinfectant since then; still, after all these years, if I see any maggots it always reminds me of that pig's head.

I do not want you to think that we did not understand that as they shared the house they were not entitled to party or to play loud music, but I am sure you will agree that when there are other people that also share the same house, there has to be understanding on both sides. The situation did not get any better over the coming months, and there were times when, after we had argued, we ended up not speaking. Now I began to dread each evening, always wondering if there was going to be another argument that night. Once again as I look back and remember it makes me feel sad, because as children there had never been any bad feelings between my sister and me. Maybe because our loyalties were now divided between each other and our husbands there was the taking of sides, and because of this, nothing could be resolved.

I think it all came to a head when finally my second baby was born. I remember it was a Saturday afternoon when Mum and Dad and my aunt and her husband were downstairs in the house that I gave birth to my second son. This time I did not go into hospital to have my baby, as I was healthy and there had been no complications with the first birth, I was able to have my baby at home, which was very common at that time. He weighed in at the same weight as his brother but where his brother had been round and chubby, he was long and slender. I remember how his dad had gotten upset because he was not the first person to see him. For some reason the midwife had allowed Mum and Dad and aunt and uncle into the bedroom first to see the new arrival. This was another memory for him that he never forgot, and I knew by the way he often spoke about it over the years that the hurt must have always remained with him.

That same evening when my sister and brother-in-law came home, they decided to have their friends over, and when the midwife returned to check on me at the end of the day and heard the noise that was going on, she was not at all happy; it was not long after she went back downstairs that the music stopped and all was quiet. (Hooray for midwives).

I am not sure how long after that situation had occurred that, on a Saturday evening when we arrived home from spending the afternoon with Mum and Dad, as we opened the front door we knew that not all was right. As we walked towards the kitchen, we saw that the sink unit had been ripped out and the china sink which had been left out in the garden after it was replaced was now resting on bricks under the tap. Then when we looked around the rest of the house, we saw that the rooms that had been occupied by them were now empty. They had decided to move without telling us, but I think what upset me the most was when I went into **my sons'** bedroom and found that they had emptied his small wardrobe that they had given him, leaving all his clothes in his cot and taken the wardrobe with them. They did leave us a note to say that they were leaving the cooker till we were able to get another one (funny I don't remember at all what happened to that cooker), but then it suddenly hit me that we were now going to be solely responsible for paying the rent - but how on earth would we be able to do that.

Once again I knew that the future was looking bleak, for there was no way that we would be able to pay the rent on the wages he received. He decided that he would approach the owners to see if there could be any solution to this, but of course he knew the rent was our problem, not theirs; they could always find another tenant, but nevertheless, he said he would try.

Over the next few weeks we struggled to pay the rent, which took most of our money; he had been to see the landlord but had been told that there was no way that he could help with our situation. Because of all the tension, the atmosphere between us became difficult, and then when I thought that things could not get any worse, he walked in one evening after work and said that he had lost his job. Now it was not just the fear of loosing my home, but there was no job either, which meant there would be no money coming in. I can't remember what the reason for loosing his job was, but as I write, I can feel the churning of my stomach that I must have felt that evening as he told me, and somehow the panic that I felt then I feel now. I now have a roof over my head, and I have no small children, but the feeling of dread is still there, for in my mind, I am not at my table writing this, but back in that house walking from room to room frightened of what the future holds for me and my babies; frightened because we have nowhere to go.

I remember on going to see Mum and Dad, but they could not think of any solution to our problem, and what they thought of the situation that we had been left with I cannot remember. As I write I am trying to put myself in their shoes, knowing how difficult it is at times to understand why brothers and sisters do the things they do to each other and knowing how difficult it is for parents not to take sides with their children.

He now began to look for new employment, as we were desperate for him to start work. So from early morning till the evening the following week, he stayed out trying to find a job, but came home at the end of each day with the look on his face which told me there was nothing. The money from his last pay packet was almost gone, so we made the decision to see if it would be any easier for me to get employment till he was able to do so. All I could get was a job in a small factory working the evening shift, but at least this way he would still be able to look for work during the day, and we would have at least some money coming into the house. There is hardly anything I remember about this place of employment; all I recall is working a large loom, so it must have been in a factory that dealt in cotton.

Soon the days were turning into weeks, and he had still not found any employment. Then one morning when we opened a letter, staring at us was the words "Notice to Quit." Where was that light at the end of the tunnel that every one talks about, I ask myself as I write, and still have that churning in my stomach as I remember. What was I going to do now? Once again I have no home. Will this road I am travelling ever not be full of obstacles? We had tried everything we could, but you cannot make people give you work, and you cannot make people give you a roof over your head

It had been two days since we had moved out of the house in Perivale and because we still had not found anywhere to live, we stayed with Mum and Dad, but because there was hardly any room in the flat he had slept in Dad's car for the two nights.
This brought the situation to a head; we had to do something, but what? I cannot remember how the idea of living in a caravan came up, but soon we were looking through a magazine which showed residential sites where caravans could be rented - the only problem was that the nearest site was situated near Newbury in Berkshire.

Part 8.

NEWBURY

We were soon on the phone speaking to the person who rented out the caravans. He told us that he had several to let, and when we asked him how much they were to rent for, he said it was according to the size as to how much he charged. We told him that we would need a four-berth, and after telling us the details, he ended with saying that we would have to pay a month in advance. I can't remember how much the rent each week was, but I do know that finding the month in advance was our next problem. Of course we never told him this, and just said that we would be there as soon as we could. Now the question was: how were we going to get the month's rent in advance besides having enough money to live on till he was able to find work? We talked all this over with my Mum and Dad, and even though they were not happy, as it meant moving away, they knew that it was the only way of solving our accommodation problem. We also told them about having to find a month's rent in advance besides money to live on till he was able to get work. They said they could help with some of this but not all. So what did I do? I got the bus and went back to the pawn shop, and pawned my engagement ring. But there was still not enough money, so he said he would go to his older brother and ask if he could help with a loan, which we would pay back as soon as he got a job - but his brother said no.

Even though we were not sure how we would manage, we knew we had no choice but to go, as the most important thing at this time was to have a roof over our heads. We knew as long as we had enough money to take care of the children and pay the month's rent, we would somehow manage to live on the little bit that was left. But inside me I was praying that it would not be too long before he found work. Where is this road taking me and will it ever come to an end?

As I write, I see myself living in a four-berth caravan on a large field at Greenham Common. Dad drove us there, which made it far easier than getting a train, and after unloading the car and watching him drive away, the apprehension inside of me was growing, as I had no idea what living in a caravan was going to be like. As I look out of the window, I see rows of caravans of all different sizes. Some you know are empty just by looking at them, as they look so dark and cold; others have a warmth about them, as their lights are glowing in the dark, which gives a feeling of comfort - but I have tears in my eyes, and my heart is heavy. There is no time to feel sorry for myself, though, as I have children to feed, and beds to make as he starts to unpack our few belongings. What did we do with our furniture? I ask myself as I write, but I don't remember.

The next morning as I looked out and saw a field of caravans I asked myself "what am I doing here?" The night before it all looked so different, but in the cold light of day the look of comfort had gone and as I looked around I found myself wondering about the other people living on this field. Are they here because they choose to be, or are they here because they to have no choice, just like me?

Now: a little information about Greenham Common. This is an area that was known in the 1960s for the American airbase that was stationed there. Where at night we would lay in bed and here the roar of the engines, and later, by the 1980s, it became better known for a Woman's Peace Camp that had been set up in protest against the reason the airbase was there; today that is all gone.

At the top of the field is what I can only describe as a shed-come-shop - at least that is how I remember it - where food items are sold at a very expensive price, and because the nearest town is a bus ride a way (Thatcham, I think), we have no choice but to buy there.

We had not been here long before he managed to find work, but no matter how hard I try to remember, I cannot tell you what type of work it was, but at least at this time we had a roof over our heads and there was money coming in. Even so, by the time we paid the rent and food there was not a lot left over, and we were still struggling. The children were growing, and their needs were different, but if there was any going without, it was never them but him and me. I remember once when it was pouring with rain there was shopping to get, so putting the children in a pram, I pushed them over the field which squelched beneath my feet, and when I returned to the caravan waiting there was my Mum and Dad. How glad I was to see them! It seemed ages since Dad had driven away. Soon we were sitting drinking cups of tea, when Dad said "what's that on your feet?" and when I looked down, my feet were black. When he bent and lifted them up, he saw the big holes I had in the soles of my shoes, which I had tried to cover up by putting cardboard inside, but because of walking across a wet field, the cardboard had become sodden and had allowed the water to get in, and so, in turn, had come up into the shoe and had made my feet look black.

This was the only time in my life that I saw my Dad with tears in his eyes, trying not to cry. Now there is another feeling going on inside of me - one that I had never experienced before, one that is making me feel guilty - that I had brought my Dad to this. He got up from where he was sitting and went outside, and as I saw him standing there, I looked at Mum not knowing what to do, and again, as I remember, I ask myself 'what must have been going through his mind.' He would remember me as I was: a carefree teenager, someone who never wanted for shoes.

He was not out there long when he came back into the caravan and told me to get my coat and asked Mum to take care of the boys while he took me into Newbury to buy a pair of shoes. I remember sitting very quietly on the journey, not really knowing what to say, and then feeling embarrassed in the shop having to watch my Dad pay for the shoes.

This story has made me look back and remember the times when, as children, we needed shoes but there was not always enough money to buy new ones, so Dad would buy pieces of leather which would come in different sizes; if it was from a cobbler's, he would buy this, or from somewhere else I do not remember, but from the cupboard he would take out a cobbler's last, which was made of metal, divided in to three parts and joined together; at each end there was shaped the pattern of a foot, each one being a different size. He would then slip the shoe onto the foot and, as I remember, I can see him now with a hammer in his hand, tacking the piece of leather onto the sole of the shoe, and then with a sharp knife, shape the leather to the sole. Then, with ball-wax, smear this around the outside of the sole. It's funny how one memory can trigger another.

At first living in the caravan felt that we were on holiday, as it reminded me of some of the caravan holidays that I had been taken as a child, but as time went on, the caravan seemed to get smaller the longer we were living in it, and I know I could not have been happy, as many times I would suddenly have the urge to leave, and the next minute the children and I would be on a train going back to Ealing to stay with Mum and Dad, just leaving a note saying I would return in a few days, hoping the break from the caravan would help me settle for a while longer. But now there was another surprise: I was pregnant again!

We knew there was no way that we could live in a caravan with three children, so I phoned my Mum at work and asked if she and Dad could come to the caravan, as we needed to talk to them. On one hand I wanted to see them, but at the same time I was worried at what they would say about another baby on the way. They arrived on Friday evening, and when I told them that I was pregnant, and that we wanted to move back to London, they just looked at each other. As I write, here I am again wondering what must have been going through there minds. There I was, with two small children and with another baby on the way, and still with no proper home, still not settled, and still struggling. Did they know what the future held for me, I wonder?

When they left that evening he went with them, saying he would use the weekend to try and find us a place. What was I thinking while I was on my own? The children kept me busy during the day, but what about the times when they were sleeping and the night, which seemed to go on forever. Watching the clock, the hands seemed not to move. All is quiet, and there is not a sound and once again I ask myself: is it always going to be like this? Will the sun never shine for me?

On the Sunday evening when he returned with my Dad, he said that he had managed to find us a furnished flat through an agency, and that we were to pack up everything and go back with my Dad that night. I couldn't believe it! "How did you manage to find a place so soon" I ask him? Imagine how I felt! No longer would I be living in a caravan, we would be settled at last. I could not control the excitement in me. The sun was starting to shine. We began packing up all our belongings and drove back to stay the night at Mum's, looking forward to moving into the flat the following day.

The next morning he left early to collect the key from the agency. I kept looking out the window, waiting for him to return, all the time wondering what the flat would be like. Was it small? How many rooms did it have? Did it have a garden where the children could play? So many questions going round and round in my head. He had been given very little information, as it was new even to the agency. Soon I saw him crossing the road towards the house. I ran down the stairs to open the door before he had a chance to ring the bell, but when I opened the door, I knew straight away from the look on his face that there was some thing wrong. "What's wrong?" I say, but he doesn't say a word while he climbs the stairs. The joy I had felt only a few moments ago has gone, and now is replaced with a feeling of sickness in my stomach. What now, I say to myself. We have been refused the flat, he says. Why I ask? Because when they realised we had children they changed there mind about letting it to us he says. Surely the agency told them we had children, I say - why didn't they tell them about the children? I kept saying, as once again I am in tears not knowing what we are going to do? They want me to go back to the agency later this afternoon, he says. Meanwhile, they will try and find somewhere else, but as they feel responsible for the situation, if nothing is found, we can stay with them.

So now I am praying hard that they will find something, as there is no way I wanted to live with strangers again, even if it is only for a short while. Later that same evening, after he had left for the agency, he returned in a car driven by the agent. He told me that they had managed to find a place in Chiswick, but it was only one room, as this was all that could be found at such short notice - but at least the landlady was willing for us to stay, even though we had children.

Part 9.

CHISWICK

One room, I hear you say. I felt the same way as you are now. How was I going to manage with three children in one room? That's if the landlady would allow us to stay once I had my new baby? But I could not worry about that now; at least we had somewhere to live for the time being. But first I must tell you about the house, the people that lived there, and the room that we lived in.

The house is quite a distance from the main shopping area of Chiswick. It has a path leading to the front door, and to the right of this there is a small garden. As you enter the house there is a door to the right, then facing you a passage that leads to stairs, which take you to the first landing. To the right of the stairs there is another small passage leading to a kitchen at the back of the house, which is used mainly by the landlady. After climbing about 15 stairs there is a landing with three doors leading off. The first opens into the landlady's bedroom; the second opens into the bathroom, and the third to the lavatory. From here, you turn and climb a few more stairs to another landing where there are two more doors facing you. The one to your left is a room occupied by another tenant, and the door to the right opens to the room where we will live. Turning once again, there are more stairs which lead to an attic room, also occupied by another tenant.

I can still see the room so clearly, it's as if I am standing at the open door looking in. I see a bay window over looking the street below, and as I take my first step inside, I see a large wardrobe to the right; beyond this is a double bed which takes up most of the wall. Under the bay window is a small wooden table, and as I look I can see and hear the television that is resting on this. Then as I look again, there is a fireplace which stands out with alcoves on either side. In the first alcove there is a small cooker (which has just two rings for cooking) resting on a small table, and in the second, a large chest of draws. The room is meant to be heated by a gas fire, but it's not this that is burning, but the oil fire that we bought when we were living in our first little room. Behind the door there is a single bed where the boys are sleeping, one at the top, and the other at the bottom; in the middle of the room sits a large round wooden table with chairs pushed underneath, and the floor I see is covered with a large carpet that must be old as the pattern has faded. The rent we paid for this room, I remember was five pounds per week, which at the time was a lot of money. There are so many things I remember about the days I lived here - how can I tell you about them all? I could write a book just on this part of my life. So I will tell you about just a few, and this will give you an idea of how it was.

The lady who owned the house seemed very old to me at the time, and each Monday when the rent had to be paid, it was her son (not her) who would knock on our door. He never lived in the house, but each Monday evening we would hear his car pull up outside, and then not long after hear the sound of his feet on the stairs. The next sound was of him knocking, and then speaking to the man in the room next to ours. A minuet later he would knock our door. We would pay the rent and then he would be gone, climbing the next set of stairs to the attic room. Then in no time at all, we would hear his car start up and he would drive away. We often wondered why he never seemed to spend a lot of time with his mother - it was as if he had no interest in staying other than to collect the rents. I remember he always seemed so miserable, never smiling and never wanting to spend any longer than was necessary talking to any of the tenants. But on one occasion when a water leak was found in the attic, and knowing there was a plumber in the house, he knocked on our door and asked him if he would fix it. Draining down the system and then mending the leak turned out to be a much bigger job than was first thought, and when it came to presenting him with the cost, we had no idea of how much to charge, so it was decided between us to ask for the amount of one week's rent. The look on his face when the price was given to him told us that he thought this was far too much, but he paid it anyway, so that week we had a little more to spend.

I think though what I remember most about the lady who owned the house is the many times I would have to rush downstairs to her sitting room to tell her there was the smell of burning coming from her kitchen. I would knock on her sitting room door and find her quite happily in her chair watching television, completely unaware of any danger, and it was only when I told her of the smell did she suddenly remember that the cooker was being used. So maybe this was one of the reasons why her son came each week to collect the rent. He was probably worried that she would forget where she put the money, or if she had even collected the rent at all, but at least we had been given a rent book so this was not something we were concerned about.

Eventually I had no choice but to tell her about the new baby coming, and I remember being very nervous, almost having the baby then and there, afraid her words would be 'you must leave.' After what seemed an eternity, she smiled and said we could stay and then asked the question 'but how will you manage in one room?' I will manage, I say knowing I had no choice. At least for the time being we never had the worry of trying to find another place to live before the baby was due.

There were two other tenants occupying the house - an elderly man in the room next to ours, and a young woman who lived in the attic room. I often met them as we passed on the stairs and they would spend a few minutes talking with the boys. I remember that the man had a lady friend who he often spoke about, giving me the impression that he was fond of her, but the young woman only ever spoke about the people she worked with, and seemed to spend most evenings and even weekends on her own, but it was not long before I brought a smile to her face for when she held my new baby in her arms - I'm sure her joy almost matched mine. The baby this time was a girl, so you can imagine how thrilled we were after having two boys. She weighed in at just one ounce heavier than her brothers, but all was fine - she had all her fingers and toes. She was born in West Middlesex Hospital, just like her older brother, and once again as I remember, I can hear myself quietly singing to her as I cradle her in my arms.

On the day that she was born we had been invited to dinner with the girl I had been to school with - the one who had always liked dancing, just like me. She was married now and living in a flat close to Chiswick High Street. We always thought it was such a coincidence that we should end up living so close to each other, but life is full of coincidences. I have tried hard to remember how it was that we had met up again, but I just cant'; I do remember after we had eaten our Sunday lunch and started to watch a program on television called "Sunday Night at The London Palladium" with a part in it called Beat the Clock, an ambulance had to be called for me. (I never did get to see who beat the clock!)

Even though we were grateful in having found a landlady prepared to rent to us, living in one room was not easy. To get drinking water I had to go to the kitchen downstairs. I remember I had a tall enamel jug that I would have to keep filling. About a fortnight before my baby was due I was struggling down the stairs, jug in one hand and with the boys holding onto me, I lost my footing and bounced down the stairs, and when I reached the bottom I just sat there not wanting to move, and with both children frightened and crying - that was another day that I was glad when it came to an end, but doing the laundry was the most difficult. I would take the cloths down to the bathroom and wash them in the bath, hoping that the other tenants would not want to bathe before I had time to finish, but then the only place I had to dry them was in the room where we were living. Whether there were other tenants before us who had done the same thing I did not know, but the walls of the room were very damp, so when the children were put to bed at night we would first pull the bed away from the wall so the boys would not roll into it in their sleep. On the occasions when I could afford it, I would take the washing to the launderette in the town. How did I cope, I am asking myself as I write? Was it because I was much younger, or maybe because I never expected anything different?

He had managed to get work not long after we had moved to Chiswick, and as far as I can remember, I am sure it was with the Pyreen Company on the Great West Road, Brentford. This was a factory once again designed in Art Deco by Wallis, Gilbert and Partners between 1929 and 1930 and would stand out for its great architecture.

Even though he now had a regular job, money was still very short; on one occasion when I visited my aunt, she told me of a factory warehouse where, if you took clothes made mainly from wool, they would buy these from you. So it was not long before I visited my aunt again with the intention of going to the warehouse. I had looked amongst our clothes and the children's that they had grown out of for any that were made from mainly wool, and I can still remember the butterflies I had in my stomach at the thought of visiting this place.

I cannot describe this building to you, as the only memory I have is standing at a counter and feeling the embarrassment while watching my bag of clothes being emptied by a woman on the other side. She began to separate the items in to two piles, which I soon realised would be the ones she would keep and the ones that would be returned. I remember the feeling of embarrassment - even now it is overwhelming at the thought that I had come down to this. I remember not being able to look the woman in the face as she separated the cloths, and then holding my hand out for the few coins that were put there. Why, I ask myself, did I ever return to the warehouse? But I know travelling on that road gave me no choice.

How much I was paid for the cloths that they kept, or how often I visited the warehouse I do not remember, but I know it was the first place I thought of when money was needed, as I never did redeem my engagement ring. Thinking and writing about this has brought tears to my eyes - did I really do this I am asking myself. (Time to make a cup of tea).

I continued to visit my school friend, and one day when I arrived she was all excited. She told me that her husband had managed to get a job in the new town of Harlow in Essex, which even though had been built for a number of years, was still known as a 'new' town, and with this would come a new council house. Then her next words to me were 'why you don't try to move there?' All that is needed is for him to get work, and you are bound to get a new house with three children. Once again my mind begins to work overtime - I cannot wait for him to come home. I am watching the clock, counting each minute. I was full of the idea of moving to the new town, especially if it meant we would be given a new house. I wouldn't even mind if it was old one.

Before he had even taken his coat off I was telling him my news, and he must have known by the excitement in my voice that I had already made up my mind that it was something I wanted to do. I began to make more sense to what I was saying when I had calmed down and explained to him properly what was involved. There was a long silence at first, then he said "but I have a regular job here." I know, I say, but what about the house? We can't live here forever. So, by the end of the evening the decision was made that he would visit Harlow, and if he was able to find work, we would go.

Finding a job in the new town had been easier than we had expected. I have no memory now of the work he had managed to find, but there was no waiting to see if he had been successful in getting the job, as a date to start had been given to him the same day, and when he came home and told me that he had found work and had been given a starting date I was elated. At last the road I am travelling was going to get easier; nothing, it seemed, could go wrong. He has work in a new town, and soon I will have a proper home for me and my family.

The new employer had told him that before a house could be given to us we would have to be recommended by our own local council. That's no problem I say - I will go there first thing Monday morning.

Monday morning my steps to the Council offices were full of bounce. I can see myself pushing the pram with my baby all cosy and warm, her head just showing above the blankets. My younger son is sitting on the end of the pram with his legs dangling over the end, and my older son walks bedside me, holding tight to the handle of the pram. But there was no heaviness in my heart that morning, for I would soon be living in a new town!

When I arrived I explained the situation and was soon filling out forms. They told me that one of their officers would visit us and then a follow-up letter would be sent telling us if we had been recommended.

The time of waiting was a mixture of excitement and apprehension. There was no reason I could think of why they would not recommend us, but still I would be glad when the waiting was over. Once again in my mind I had already set up home, and I could see the children playing in the garden, and then later tucked up in their own little beds that were in rooms of their own. I could see my house just waiting for us.

It was a Saturday morning that we had our visit. We invited the man into our room, and he sat and spoke to us for a while, asking us all sorts of questions. All the time I could feel my heart beating, asking myself if these are the answers he wants I offered him a cup of tea, but he refused, and somehow that made me feel uncomfortable but I was not sure why. I remember it was very difficult trying to talk to him with the children there, as they did not understand, and they wanted us to talk to them and not him. When he had finished filling out the forms he had with him, we asked if he could tell us if we were recommended, but he said no, it was not up to him. He said we would get an answer by post, but when he left a voice inside of me kept telling me that the interview had not gone well, and I wished that we could have it all over again. I wanted so much for this road I was travelling to change. Surely the sun must shine soon.

The starting date for the new job was not far away and we still had not received the Council's letter. Every day I looked for the postman, rushing down the stairs, hoping it would be there on the mat. He had decided not to give in his notice to leave his job at Pyreen, just in case something did go wrong, and I was beginning to feel that this had been a good decision. Then at last the letter arrived. I could barely bring myself to open the envelope, wondering what was written inside. It will be alright, I say to myself, still with that little niggle inside. Then as I began to read the words, the ones that stood out the most were "Sorry" and "Unsuccessful."

Once again my dreams had been shattered. All of the things I had seen in my imagination were no more, and there was nothing to replace them, and for the rest of the day all I could think of was what might have been, and held back the tears till he walked through the door. We decided that I would phone the Council offices the following day to ask why they had refused to recommend us, but when I did this, all they would say was "we are unable to tell you, that is our policy."

As I write now, I am thinking to myself how different the road I was travelling might have been if someone in those Council offices had made a different decision. It has made me wonder how many of us stop and think of the consequences of a judgement made when there are other peoples lives involved, and now, because of their decision, travelling on this road only becomes harder, for now I see myself working in the offices of a factory in Brentford. The town of Brentford is the same town that I described to you earlier, but why and how the decision to go back to work came about I do not remember; I can only think that because of the continued shortage of money, this is what tempted me back into the workplace and so the road I am travelling begins to go yet again in another direction.

I managed to get the children settled into a day nursery run by the local council; my working day would start about 9AM and finish about 5PM, which seems all very straight forward, but what really went on behind that sentence was much harder. Trying to get three young children washed, dressed and with something warm inside them before leaving home early in the morning was not easy, and because catching a train to Brentford was much quicker than going by bus, I would have to make sure that I was at the station on time so as not to miss the train that would get me to Brentford with time to settle the children into the nursery and then make my way to my work - but the walk to the station was not just five minutes away, and as I was pushing a heavy push chair with three children on it - the baby on the seat, then my oldest son leaning over her, holding onto the handle with his feet resting on the pram, and then my other son standing on the back of the pushchair holding onto the side of the handle, with me leaning over him, pushing the pram - there were times I would be worn out before I even started my day's work! When the weather was fine pushing the pram was a little easier, but on the mornings when it was either foggy, raining, snowing or just plain cold, there were times when I just wanted to turn around and go back home. I ask myself how did I do it, but as it became routine to get the same train each day, the other passengers began to help me as I struggled morning and evening to get the children and the push chair on and off the train

Leaving the children at the nursery was not easy for me, as

sometimes they would cry, and this would give me a feeling of guilt at having to walk away from them, but I was always assured that not long after I left they would begin to play with the other children, and would soon settle down into the routine of the nursery. The walk from the nursery to my place of work did not take me long, but I have no recollection of what this company was called; I only see myself sitting at a desk with a typewriter resting on it, in an office that is filled with people. How long I stayed working for this company I am not sure, but my memories of working there are only good.

As I have told you, the town of Brentford is very old and is known for the many famous people that have lived there, but for me this town is remembered for something quite different - it is the times in winter when, after work and before I collected the children, I would visit the shops, wondering what to buy for dinner each night. It is not just that I remember Brentford for, but how, in winter, the lights from the shop windows would light up the pavement, and as I see myself walking through this small town, I feel the warmth that somehow my memory is giving me as I remember the shops with their lights glowing in the dark.

The disappointment of not moving to the new town stayed with me for a while, as I kept thinking of what might have been, and when my friend finally moved from her flat in Chiswick, we promised each other that we would keep in touch, but once again because of time and unforeseen circumstances, promises are not always kept.

As the children were growing, the time had come for us to look around for somewhere else to live. Once again I visited the Council offices, this time to see if they would allocate us a council house, but they said that their housing list was full, and it would be many years before they could house us. Each Saturday he would spend as much time as he could, searching notice boards and visiting estate agents once again. A bigger place would mean more money, and as there was no chance of either of us working extra hours at our places of employment, I decided that I would take on an evening job as well as the day job. He was not very happy about this, but I felt there was no other way. It was not long before I found myself working at The White City dog track. How I found this job I do not remember, but I see myself working on what is known as the tote, sitting in a tote booth, working a machine that has a handle that turns, and me looking through a small window placing bets for the people that had come for a night out dog racing.

White City Stadium, sadly, is no longer there as in 1985 it was demolished and bought by the BBC (British Broadcasting Company), who then built their radio headquarters there, but this was a stadium that was much loved by the people of London. It was built by George Wimpy and opened in 1908 by King Edward VII for the Summer Olympics of that year. Over the years it has been the home of many sporting events, such as football, rugby, speedway racing, show jumping and dog racing, to name but a few; so perhaps many a tear was shed on its last day. Whenever I hear people speak about the stadium, it brings to mind one funny story that still puts a smile on my face.

We had closed the booth after bets had been placed for the last race, and as I had never seen greyhounds run, I went with one of the other girls to watch the race. As I stood waiting I saw two girls, each carrying a dustpan and brush, walking along the track; when I asked the question, what are they doing? In good old fashioned English, she told me. I am sure you have guessed what she said. All right, what do I know?

There was one problem I had when I decided to work at the stadium, and that was, as there was a 20 minute difference between me having to leave to catch the train and him coming home from work, I would need someone to be with the children, so I decided to ask the girl upstairs if she would sit with them till he came home, to which she

131

agreed. I did offer to pay her for this but she refused to accept any money.

Eventually we managed to find our next home: A flat, which consisted of a large bedroom a sitting room, a kitchen, and a very small bathroom at the very top of a three story house in Ealing Broadway. I had come full circle - I was back in Ealing.

Part 10.

EALING BROADWAY

Ealing, known as "The Queen of the Suburbs," but for me it is much more than that. It was my home, and no matter where I have lived, this will always be the place that, in my mind, I return to. It holds for me the memories of childhood: of Mum and Dad, Saturday morning pictures, school and parks to play. Shopping on Saturday afternoons, the place I began to fall in love, and of course my Nan. It is also a place with much history and many famous people. People like Spencer Percival, born in 1762, who became Prime Minister of England in 1809, and who was later shot in the House of Commons in 1812 by John Bellingham (who just a week later was hanged). In more modern times, there was the singer Dusty Springfield, a recording artist who sold millions of records but who sadly died in 1999; the comedian Sid James, who starred in the many "Carry On" comedy films and died in 1976. But I think one of the most outstanding landmarks of Ealing history is Ealing Studios, where many classic films were made (The Blue Lamp; It Always rains on Sunday, and The Lady Killers) - all classics today, but again, you probably have never heard of them.

Again there were other families who shared the house with us, but only two of the families I remember. The family who lived in the flat below us, and a family living in the basement; but because I was out most of the day and evening, I never really got to know them.

Living in the flat was so much easier. We still had to share the bedroom with the children, but at least we had a sitting room and a separate kitchen, and most of all, a bathroom that we never had to share with other tenants. I remember there was a large back garden that we could see if we looked out of the sitting room window, but the people who lived on the ground floor rented the garden with their flat, so we never did get to use it. I remember also that whenever the window in the sitting room needed cleaning I would first clean the inside and then I would sit on the outside ledge of the window, pull the window down on my lap and with a bottle of cleaner in one hand and a cloth in the other, I would rub away, hoping no one would say "You missed a bit" (remember this is at the very top of a three storey house). When I think of this I wonder what ever made me do that. Now I would just pretend that the dirt on the window was not there and look forward to the rain. .

Once we moved to Ealing there was no way that I could continue working two jobs, mainly because there was no one to look after the children till he came home. So it was decided that I should give up working during the day. How glad I was that no longer would I have to leave the children at the day nursery and have the awful feeling of guilt each time I left them. Now it was only catching the train each evening from Ealing Broadway Station to White City, and the station was only five minuets away, but even then on occasion I would have to run so as not to miss my train.

As soon as I gave up working during the day, I contacted my two friends who I had worked with at Bush Radio. Not only had my life changed but theirs had too. The one that reminded me of an Egyptian was now married with a little girl and lived in Richmond, and still did not own an asp; and the other, who now had two children, still lived in Acton, though in a different house. I remember I visited the first one just once then heard later that she had separated from her husband, but the other I visited several times and spent many a happy hour talking and drinking tea while the children played. There was never a hint that she was unhappy till one evening there was a knock at the front door and when we opened it, standing there was her husband who was looking for my friend, saying that she too had left taking the children with her. He asked if I knew where she would have gone, but when I said I knew nothing about why she would leave or where she would be, I felt that he did not believe me.

It was several weeks later that she too turned up on the doorstep, saying that she had now gone back to her husband, and said that they would soon be moving away. Since that day I have never heard from either of those friends again. What happened to them I am thinking now? Where did their roads take them? It's only because I have decided to write have I thought about them after all these years, and now wonder, have they ever thought about me?

Time has moved on and I am no longer working at White City, and he is no longer working at Pyrene. Again I am unable to remember the reason why he left his job or how he came to be working for a one-man pluming business, and I too must have had a reason why I chose to leave White City. I only know that once again the worry of not enough money is taking over my life, and one morning as the electric bill drops onto the door mat, and after not really wanting to open it, I say to my self 'how on earth will we pay this?' Soon it is not only the electricity that cannot be paid but the rent for the flat as well. He asked his employer if there is any overtime, but instead he finds himself only working a few days a week as there seems to be not much call for plumbers at this time.

Now everything seems to be going from bad to worse. We no longer have electricity; the flat is being lit by candlelight, as we are unable to pay the bill. Having no electric is not just having no light, but also means not being able to iron or use any other electrical item, and as my oldest son is now in school and old enough to know that all is not as it should be, this makes it very hard trying to explain to him the reason why things are like they are without worrying him. We still had the oil fire, so at least we could keep warm - that is until one day when I didn't have the money for oil and was wondering what to do when my Dad knocked on the door. When he realised we had no heat it was not long before he had been to the shop and was back again and we were warm. What would I have done with out my

Dad? Tears are in my eyes again.

At this time my sister and brother-in-law had moved to Aberdare, in South Wales and also were the proud parents of a little girl. Why they decided to move there, I don't remember but after many years they still felt that they had made the right decision in choosing to go. I know that Mum and Dad were upset when my sister left, but knew they had to make their own way in life and do what was right for them; even though there had been bad times between my sister and me, that was now all forgotten.

It was on a visit to us that they suggested that a holiday would do the children good, so when they returned home they took the children with them. The following week I was to travel to Wales and spend a few days there, and then the children and I would return home, but the week without them was not as I thought it would be as I missed them so much and could not wait to see them.

On arriving in Aberdare it was strange, as this was the town that we had been evacuated to during the war; while I was there I looked for the places that had been part of those war years. I remembered the school and the little sweet shop where I had bought my first ice cream, and the farm where I had lived which had given me such happy memories. I found the little shop and also found the school, but the farmhouse had gone and the lane where I had picked the blackberries was nowhere to be found, but I was happy I had found some of my memories and the farm house and the lane where I picked the blackberries would still always be there for me in my memories.

It was not long before the suggestion was made that we should move to Aberdare, and although the idea seemed a good one, making the decision to move away from Ealing would be far harder this time as my son was in school and doing well. Then there was my Mum and Dad to consider, as they would be left on their own, but the main question was how would he take the suggestion of moving; as there was no way I could contact him, I decided that if I found a place to live before I went home, then it would be easer for the decision to be made.

So began the task once again of looking for somewhere to live; it was not long before I had the address of a house that was for rent from an estate agent. I became very excited at the thought of moving, not only to a new house, but once again to a completely new area - but when I look back now, I ask myself was it really what I wanted. Did it only seem the right thing to do because of the situation we were in? The answer I give myself was that if things had been different, I would never have left Mum and Dad and moved away from my roots.

The understanding with the estate agent was that we would accept the house on return to Aberdare, which would be as soon as we could vacate the flat where we were living, and that was agreed. My next task was convincing him that once again we should move – this, I felt, was not going to be easy.

All the way home on the coach I was anxious as to what his reaction would be when I told him what I had been doing while away, and wondered if he would say no to moving. On arriving home, I knew that all was not right, and it was not long before I was reading a letter that had been sent to say we were being evicted because the rent had not been paid. Not only were we being evicted, but the bailiffs were being sent in. Now absolute panic took over - it was not just losing a roof over my head, but all the items that had made up my home.

Now there was no choice, we had to move, and as I told him of the house I had found, even though it meant leaving London. He did not say anything that was not positive; saying maybe this is a new start for us.

Now that the decision to move had been made for us, time spent with Mum and Dad became very precious. They were very upset that once again we were having to move away, saying this time they would not be able to visit as often as Wales was much further than Newbury, but in between the tears they again understood the reasons why we had to go.

It was a Friday morning that I stood at the end of the road and watched as all the furniture that I had was being loaded into a large van to be taken away and sold. How I must have felt as I stood and watched I can only imagine now, but as I write, once again it becomes overwhelming, and I ask myself as I did before. *Why?*

We never stayed to watch the last item being put into the van, but left and caught the train to Cardiff and from there a bus to Aberdare. On arriving at my sister's I was handed a letter from the estate agents. Soon I was tearing open the envelope all excited at the thought of the house but the first word I noticed once again was, "Sorry."

Part 11.

SOUTH WALES

I just could not believe what I was reading - it said that the owners had changed their minds about renting and had decided to sell instead, but would give us first refusal if we chose to buy the house. Buy a house what with? All the money we had consisted of a few pounds in change and a check for twelve pounds that had been given to him by his employer on his last day of work; why do I remember the amount of that check so clearly after all these years? You will find out soon, if you have not already guessed.

Once again I find myself asking 'what are we going to do now?' as there was no way that we could return to Ealing. I knew we couldn't stay with Mum and Dad, as their flat was not big enough for all of us, and besides, property for rent was much harder to find in London. While all of this was going through my mind, I heard my sister say that we could stay with them until we were able to find somewhere else to live. For that moment I felt some relief, but at the same time hoped that it would not be too long before we would find a place of our own, as I knew that living together in a flat that was just big enough for her family would soon create different problems.

As I lay awake that night I asked myself: was it only that morning that I stood and watched as my home was being loaded into a van to be taken away, and only a few days earlier he had said that a new start was around the corner. When we had started our journey that morning I really believed that the future did look better, but that seemed so long ago. As I lay with my head on the pillow, I am asking myself once again, what does the future hold, as I try so hard to be positive.

The first two places that he visited Monday morning, were the Job

Centre (though I don't think it was called that then), and then the bank. He must have had positive results from the Job Centre, as I know it was not long before he was working, though I have no recollection of where it was, but when he presented the check to the bank it bounced. He did phone his old boss about the check but he never did get the money.

Because I had stayed in Aberdare for a few days' holiday, I had become acquainted with the town, its shops and landmarks, and soon realised that the surrounding area was also known for their coal mines. I remember sitting on buses, seeing men with dark eyes that looked as if they had pencilled eyeliner to their lids; their skin marked with scars, black from where the coal dust had become part of the healing. Some times I hear the sound of breathing that told me their lungs had already begun to pay the price for working so many years underground so that people could keep warm and industry to keep going. How many of us had ever given these men a thought, let alone the credit for what they did each day, I begin to wonder. I know I never had, but as I began to learn of the life that took place in the bowels of the earth, my respect for these men began to grow.

Soon I was showing him the town with its Coliseum Theatre that opened in 1938, which was funded by the local miners, but was now owned by the Council. Then there was the statue of Griffith Rhys Jones, a famous conductor of the South Wales Choral Union who had won a competition at Crystal Palace Exhibition in 1873, which stood in the square not far from a church built 800 years ago - so even in this small town there is such a lot of history.

Two families living together in the flat was not easy. I was continually trying to keep the children from making too much noise, always glad when they were fast asleep at night, always praying that they would not do anything that could create a problem, and always feeling that I must not get in the way. As the days passed though, the tension began to grow, and I knew we had to find a place and find it soon; it was not that we did not try, it was just that finding somewhere was proving harder than we had first thought.

We had been in Aberdare for about six weeks, and still had not found a place to live. We were now becoming desperate; there was no way we could continue to stay much longer in the flat. We appreciated that it was not easy for my sister and her husband to have us there, and they needed to have their home to themselves, when my brother-in-law announced that he had found us accommodation with people he knew who owned a large house and were willing to rent us two rooms. I was pleased that we no longer had to share the flat, but once again, two rooms were not what I was hoping for. Of course there was no way we could refuse, so while my sister looked after the children we went with my brother-in-law to see what he had found for us.

The house, I remember, was built at the very top of a lane that climbed higher and higher with each step we took, till at last we came to a farm. There we crossed the farm yard, and then climbed again, till at last, in front of us stood the house surrounded by a small fence and lots of trees. I don't remember much about the rooms in the house, just that the family who lived there lived mainly in the front sitting room and used a large kitchen at the back of the house with their bedrooms upstairs. We were shown the two rooms that we were to rent: one large room downstairs at the back of the house and one bedroom upstairs. Whether I thought of the lane I would have to climb each time I went out, or the farm yard I had to cross, I do not remember, for all of that was soon forgotten when I was told that the house had no mains water, no gas, and no electricity. The toilet was yards away from the house, where the sewage would have to be emptied after digging a hole. The water, I was told, came from a stream that ran nearby, and candles would have to be used to light the rooms at night. Even the caravan had running water, electricity and a toilet, I must have thought, but we knew we had no choice but

141

to accept the offer of the two rooms.

Did I really live with no mains water, no electricity and no gas? Did I really live like that with three children? Now, once again, I ask myself - how did I do it, and as I write and remember, wondering if it is time to make another cup of tea. (What would we do without our cup of tea)?

The family that we shared the house with made our lives as comfortable as possible, and I felt at times that they understood that it was not easy for us to live the way they were used to. The family consisted of the mum and dad and three children, all older than mine, but all the children got on well, so that at least made life easier. Now that we were settled, my next job was finding a school for the boys.

The school they began attending was some distance away from where we lived, and the journey each morning was not something that the children and I looked forward to. The head teacher felt that the boys were not old enough to stay for school dinners, which meant that I would have to make the journey eight times a day - back and forth in the morning, back and forth to pick them up dinner time, back and forth taking them back after dinner, then back and forth at the end of the school day. Doing this five days a week soon began to be far too much, not just for the children, but for me as well. After doing this for about two weeks, I explained to the head teacher that this situation could not go on, so it was agreed that the boys could stay in school for their dinner, which made each day a lot easier.

Living how we did at this time was not easy; I had known what it was like to have to carry water and be with out electricity in the past, but never dreamt that I would go down that same road again, yet somehow this did not make any difference On top of all this, it seemed that each time we left the house, one of the children would fall over crossing the farm yard, which would mean scraped knees and mucky clothe - clothes that would have to be washed in a bowl and ironed with a flat iron that I heated up on the fire or the Calor gas cooker (that we decided to buy rather than share the family's). As I ironed the clothes, I was reminded of how, years earlier, I had watched as his mother too had ironed this way, never dreaming that just a few years later I would be doing the same thing.

I have one particular memory that stands out while we lived here: We were in the middle of winter and we had taken the children to a cinema in the evening; while we were there, snow had begun to fall. At first the children were very excited at the thought of walking home with snow falling around them, and they were soon stopping, making snowballs and squealing with joy, but it was not long before the excitement fell away, for as we began to climb the lane that took us home, the piercing wind had blown and made deep snowdrifts, so walking was a lot more difficult. Soon he had lifted our daughter and was carrying her on his shoulders, and with the boys holding on tight to our hands, we battled our way through the wind and the snow, all the time telling the children that everything would be alright, as we began to hear the fear in their voices. We tried assuring them that soon we would be home in the warmth, but wait a minute, have I not been down this road before? As I write, it has brought back a memory of holding on tight to a hand that got me home safely after leaving a cinema, not in snow but fog, and fearful all the same.

Over the next months we began to make new friends, and I began to settle, though I still went back to Ealing from time to time. Then one day we were told that the Council would be re-housing the family we lived with, as the house was not suitable, and because we lived in the house as well we also would be re-housed. Try to imagine how once again I felt. At last a home of my own, where we would not have to go out in all weather to use the toilet. To be able to turn the light on at night and to drink water without having to boil it first; where even ironing clothes would be a pleasure - but the question was: how long we would have to wait?

We waited and waited and still did not hear from the Council. Soon weeks began to turn into months. Then one day, friends who lived in a small village outside of town came to see us and said that they were moving from their cottage and had spoken to there landlord about us, who had said that we could take over the tenancy if we wanted to.

In that one moment, I felt my stomach turn - I could have shouted with joy! But then reality hit. What about the council house that we had been promised? Should we wait for that? Then I reasoned that we had already waited weeks without any hint of when we would move. We could still wait months. We thanked our friends and told them of the situation, and said that we would talk it over with each other and then let them know the following day what we had decided. So that is what we did, going over and over all the reasons why we should either wait or move but in the end we came up with the decision that we should move.

Part 12.

CWMBACH

It was not many days before I was turning the key and opening the door to my new home. At last I thought this was <u>mine</u>; I had a home of my own, and I held the key. The feeling of emotion that I felt as I turned on the light, even though it was daytime, was overwhelming. I remember how the children ran from room to room, up and down the stairs screaming and laughing with joy; but this time I did not have to tell them to be quiet: this was their home, and from now on they could be themselves. (Though not screaming all the time)

The cottage part of a terrace was in the village of Cwmbach (which means small valley), not far from the town of Aberdare. As you open the front door and step inside, there is a door to the right, and when you open the door facing you, a fireplace, which was centre piece to a medium sized sitting room. As you turn to the right there is a window which looks out onto a busy main road. Coming out of this room, you turn right again and walking down the narrow passage leading you to the kitchen, which is at the back of the house. The kitchen is big enough to hold a table and four chairs, a sink, the cooker (which is ours), a few cupboards, and at the end of the room there is another fireplace.

Upstairs there are two bedrooms, both quite big, but when we opened the doors to these we knew that we could use only one of them, as the other was so damp - there was no way we, or the children, could sleep in there. Returning to the front door once outside, when looking left and just a few yards away, there is a little corner shop which sells almost everything from sugar to sewing needles. I would visit the shop often, buying things I had run out of or forgotten to buy in town. I remember as you entered the shop a bell, which was fixed above the door, would ring, and then from the back of the shop an old lady would appear, always with a smile on her face, and as I stood waiting for her to fetch what I wanted, she would always talk about the children or ask me about life in London.

There are many things I remember and picture about the cottage, but if you were to ask me what I remember most it would be the quiet times I had when he was at work, the boys were in school and my daughter sleeping. I would sit with a cup of tea in my hand relaxing and watching as I had as a child; the flames dancing in the fire that glowed in the grate. Even now as I remember, I can feel the warmth of that room, and I know that the quiet times are the times we should always treasure, but it was the sitting room where we sat together in the evenings that bring another sort of treasure. I see a family sitting together, laughing and sometimes all talking at the same time, all having their stories to tell. Oh how I wish I could remember the things we spoke about, but wait a minute: there is another picture I see, of carrying lighted coals from the fireplace in the kitchen to the fireplace in the sitting room so as not to have to build a new fire. I would wrap a damp towel over my hand, then taking a shovel, filled with the coals from the kitchen fire, walk quickly to the sitting room and lay the still-hot coals in the fire grate. Then, with a sheet of newspaper held up to the open fire, hoping this would draw any wind up the chimney and praying it would not be too long before the coals would be roaring away - but at times the paper would catch a light, and I would have to quickly scrunch it up and push it into the fire and then hunt for another sheet of newspaper and start all over again before the coals lost their heat.

Now as I remember, I ask myself, did I really do that? Did I really run from one room to another with hot coals on a shovel; and then I ask myself, would I do it now? The answer I give is, probably yes.

Having electricity now made life a lot easier as I no longer had to heat irons on a fire when doing the ironing or burn candles to give us light, and also because we had electricity what took pride of place was a television standing in the corner of the sitting room, which we all enjoyed watching. I remember when my brother-in-law visited and saw the television his first words were, "I knew that that would be the first thing you would have." (How right he was!!!)

So began a time when I felt that at last the road I was travelling was beginning to get a little easier. He had a regular job, which meant that money was coming in, so at least all the bills could be paid. The boys, no longer attending the school in the town but the village school, had soon settled down and seemed happy and my daughter was still content to be at home with me as, never once did she ask to go to school with the boys. But I think that the times the children would run to the little shop with pennies in their hands for sweets was always a time of excitement, as I can see them now all running to see who would get there first, and as I remember, it's the squeals of joy I hear, as they never left with out something extra: a lollypop that the old lady always seemed to give them. I did ask my daughter when writing this part of the book if she remembered anything about living in the cottage, and the first thing that came to her mind was the old lady that gave her the lollypops! Writing this part of my story has reminded me of another embarrassing situation which I must tell you about.

I had been out for the evening, though now I don't remember where, and to get back home I had to catch a bus. I remember that it was cold and pouring with rain, and so was glad when the bus arrived, as I couldn't wait to get home to the warmth. Soon I was ringing the bell to let the driver know that it was at the next stop I wanted to get off. The bus stopped, but as I stepped off the bus and on to the pavement I tripped and landed head first into a deep puddle. No sooner I touched the ground I was back up on my feet. I was soaking wet and wishing the bus would move on, for even though I was not hurt my dignity was. Soon I was running across the road and knocking on the door of the cottage, and when it was opened by him and as he saw me standing there dripping from a mixture of rain and coal dust running down my face he said "What the *hell* have you done?"

So as I wrote earlier, all seemed to be going well, but it was only a few weeks after we had moved into the cottage that after I had taken the boys to school and returned home, there was a knock at the door. When I opened it, standing there was a man with a clipboard in his hand, and the first thing he said was the name of my friend who had lived there before us. When I explained that she had moved and we had now taken over the tenancy, his first words were "I am from the local Council, and you should not have moved in as the cottages were due to be pulled down." In that one moment my whole world once again crashed around me, and I saw myself walking the streets looking on notice boards, hoping to find somewhere to live, but all I said was "I know nothing about the cottage being pulled down." Soon he was asking how many were in the family; wanting to know names and dates of birth, writing these down on the forms that were attached to his clipboard. Then all he said as he turned and walked away was "I will get back to you".

What are we going to do now, was all I kept thinking. I thought this at least would be my home for a little while. Maybe we could go back to the farm house, I thought, but then would that be fair for the family who lived there, as we had chosen to leave? All I wanted was for him to come home from work and to share the worry that I now felt, but each minute seemed like an hour, and each hour like a lifetime.

At last I heard the key turning the lock in the front door. As he walked into the kitchen and looked at me, he must have known there was something wrong, but before the question was asked I began to tell of the visit I had had from the man from the Council, and when I had finished I asked "what are we going to do?"

All that night all we talked about was the situation that once again we found ourselves in, wishing we had not made the decision to leave the farm house; but after all the talking it was decided that we would do nothing until we heard from the Council.

But, doing nothing was not easy for me! Now all I could think of was the "what if's". I no longer had that feeling of security. Once again, in one sentence, that had all been taken away. I felt that I should be looking on notice boards and visiting estate agents. I kept wondering how much time would there be before they would tell us that we had to move out. How long would I have to find another place to live? Would it mean that the children would have to start another school? All these questions kept going round and round in my head, and even though I wanted to know, I was frightened of the answers. I am waiting for the knock at the door, or the letter that falls on the mat. (Haven't I been down this road before)?

It was a Tuesday morning when I received the letter. I had taken the boys to school, and when I arrived back home, lying on the mat was the letter that again I did not want to open. I remember balancing the envelope on the mantelpiece above the fire, then deciding to make a cup of tea before mustering the courage to read what was inside, but I know you are wondering and saying to yourself: how does she remember it was a Tuesday? (Soon all will be revealed).

As I sipped my tea, still looking at the envelope, it all became too much. I couldn't wait any longer, so as I tear open the envelope, the first sentence I read tells me to go to the housing department in the Council offices. So I still do not know what is in store for us.

Because it is Tuesday, this is the day that I collect my Family Allowance (or child benefit), from the post office. Family Allowance was introduced by the government of the day in 1945 to help with child poverty, which most families looked forward to collecting each week, as this money would help till payday. So I decided that I would go to the post office first, and then to the Council office.

Once inside the Council office, I remember sitting on a bench that was just outside the door which was about to open onto the next part of my journey, even though I did not want to know where this road would take me. (Hold on, the door is opening.) Please come in, a voice says, have a seat. I sit down on the chair that stands in front of the desk, my heart pounding, not wanting to hear what the voice is saying. My daughter sits on my lap; can she feel the beating of my heart? Now the voice is standing up and walking towards a large map that hangs on the wall. "We are offering you a house in Cwmbach which has just been built." One of many on a new housing estate, the voice says, and then asks the question "Will you accept it?" Next he is giving me a piece of paper and telling me to take it to the site office on the new estate and then I will be shown the house that will be mine.

At first I could not believe all the things that had been said to me. I asked myself had I heard right; had I just been offered a **new** house? Had I been asked if I would accept it? I had a piece of paper in my hand that told me it was all true. The excitement I now felt was overwhelming, and I had to tell someone, but I couldn't tell him, as there was no way I could get in touch; but I could tell my Mum, I could phone her at work. So with my daughter in her pushchair, I run back to the post office where, outside, stands the phone box, and soon I am telling all about the new house and Mum so excited for me says "I can't wait to come and see it."

Now **I** can't wait to get back to Cwmbach. I decide I must go home first to give my daughter something to eat, and then my next stop will be my new home. So with my best foot forward I am marching to the bus stop. I fold the pushchair, ready for when the bus arrives, and then feel in my bag for my purse so I can pay the driver, but I cannot feel the purse. Now I am kneeling down with my bag on the ground, taking everything out, hoping it will be there. Where can it be? Where did I have it last? I am in a panic, and then I remember that the phone box was the last place I opened it, and so I realise that in

150

my excitement, I must have left it there. I see myself running, pushing the pushchair as fast as I can back to the phone box, all the time praying that my purse will still be there, and before I even have the door open, my eyes are looking through the small windows, but even after my searching it is nowhere to be found. Now you know why I remember that it was a Tuesday.

Getting home took me longer than I had expected, as now I had to walk, and whether the excitement of the house overtook the concern of how we would get through the week without the help of the family allowance I do not remember. I only see myself pushing the pushchair up a steep hill to the housing estate that was built near the top of a mountain at the back of the cottage.

When I arrived at the new housing estate, there was mud everywhere, as the site was not yet finished. There were rows of newly built houses, and flats with some already occupied; others like mine, empty, waiting for their new families. Soon the site agent was turning the key to let me in to my new home and, after showing me around the house, we made our way back to the front door, but I did not want to leave - I wanted to look around once again, but this time on my own. So I said I would look around again, giving the excuse for this as to the amount of curtains I would need; I said I would return the key to the site office on leaving.

Now I began to *really* see what the house was like. As I walked through the front door, to my left was a room with two large windows looking out onto a road at the front of the house. It had a fireplace on the wall facing the windows, but this was no ordinary fireplace, for it was all enclosed with fire proof glass in a door which could be opened and the fire made in the grate. It had a boiler built into the back of the fire, which would heat the domestic water and the radiators in each room. (Radiators! Are these really what I am seeing)? At the end of the room and to the right there was a door which took you into a small dining room; this too had a radiator, and when you looked out of the window of this room (which was the back of the house), you saw not only the garden but a very large field, and trees that led up to the mountain behind the house; dividing the garden from the field was a high wire fence. You would then leave the dining room by another door which led you to a kitchen, where there was a sink unit and a large cupboard which could be used for a pantry (somewhere to store food), and still another radiator. Then going out of the door at the other side of the kitchen would lead you to a small passage with a back door to your left, which opened onto a small yard with steps that you climbed to the garden. The yard also had a small shed that was built onto the side of the house which was used for keeping coal. To take you out of the yard to the front of the house, there was a small gate that opened onto a narrow alley, but if you didn't want to go out the back way, you would turn right as you left the kitchen, passing a door to your left, which opened onto a toilet, then facing you the front door.

In between the kitchen and the sitting room there were stairs built in the middle of the house that took you to a landing where there were five doors. To the left the first opened on to the main bedroom; the second to a much smaller bedroom known as a "box room." Facing you, an airing cupboard, and then to the right of this the bathroom, and then another bedroom.

As I walked from room to room, I felt as if I had to pinch myself to see if all of this was real or was I just dreaming, and when I finally left the house and shut the door behind me as I walked away I looked back and asked my self 'is that really mine?' as I still could not believe that at last I had the house I had always dreamed of.

I collected the boys from school and enjoyed telling them all about the new home that they would soon be living in, and could not wait for him to come home from work to tell him the good news. Was it only that morning that the postman had delivered the letter? So much had happened in that one day! I had opened a letter, been given a house, phoned my Mum, and lost my purse. (Oh, what a day)!

It was only a few days after we had been given the key to the new house that we moved in. Again the children ran from room to room in their excitement. I remember when, at the end of that day, after all the hard work of moving, when the children were tucked up in their beds how the feeling of contentment came over me. I hoped that this would be the place that we at last would be able to settle, and the children would stay till each of them decided to marry. My long term outlook was never to move again, and I really believed that life could now only get better.

It was not long before I was making new friends, first with the family who lived next door, and later with a family who lived just a few doors away, but it was the family that lived a few doors away with whom I became the closest to. Even the children seemed happy and settled, spending time with their children, and because their Dad was a coal miner, I remember how they would sit, fascinated, listening to the stories they were told of life down the mine. Now as I write, it has brought back the times when they played in the street and I would have to go looking for them when it was nearly time for bed, as they had decided to go walk about, and how they always seemed to have a good excuse for not staying close to home. In winter when the snow covered the ground, how throwing snowballs at each other became there favourite pastime, or rolling the snowballs till they grew so big they could not push them any more. But as I write and remember, am I really seeing them, or is it a reflection of me, as if time has stood still, for I say to them when they stand by the fire wet and cold from the snow "don't get too close, you will get chilblains". But they don't care either, for soon they are back outside, making more snowballs and hoping the snow will last forever; but I don't want it to last forever, as I see myself walking to my friend's with a bucket in my hand, asking if they have any small coal to spare. 'Small coal' is the word that is used for the dust that gathers amongst the coal. Miners would have a ton of coal delivered every six weeks, not for free, but at a reduced price (this is as far as I remember). I remember how a lorry would drop the coal in the road outside the house, and then it would have to be carried, a bucketful at a time to the coal shed.

So once again the situation has changed - he no longer has work, and money is in short supply, and because we have no money to buy coal, I have to ask my friend if there is any small coal to spare. When the next ton of coal is dropped by the lorry I help to carry this to the coal shed as a way of paying for the small coal that I have asked for. I see myself trying to dampen the small coal to try and make it burn longer, but I must have wet it too much, as it hardly burns at all. We need something to help it get started, so now I see us walking along a train track with carrier bags in our hands, looking for any small pieces of coal that would have dropped from the coal trucks before the line was closed, or any blocks of wood soaked in tar, hoping this would help the small coal to catch alight and burn a little longer.

How long it was before he managed to find work again I cannot recall, but now time has gone by and the children are growing up, and the next memory that comes to mind is the joy we felt when my eldest son passed his 11-plus exam. This was the same exam that I had taken when I too had been 11 years of age; though the questions would have been different, I never passed.

This exam was taken in school by children to determine there academic ability. If they passed this exam they would then go on to higher education at a grammar school, and then maybe to university, but if they failed the exam, would be educated in a secondary school where education was not so good. From here, pupils would normally start work as soon as they reached school leaving age and soon after marry.

I am trying hard to remember many of the things that took place while living in this house, like the time when looking out the window to check that the children were still where they were supposed to be that I saw, to my amazement, a very large pig running down the road with a farmer running close behind, shouting for the children to get out of the way while trying to catch it; or the time when the children's ball was taken by a very irate man who lived at the end of the road, but after a visit to his house the ball was given back; or the time we came home one evening and found that the house had water running down the stairs as a tap had been left on and the plug, still in the sink; and the time when the children could hear a funny noise in their bedroom and after a long investigation, realised that it was cows that were chewing by the fence that divided the back garden from the field. But the time that stands out the most as I remember is the time when, on this particular morning, pulling back the curtains in the sitting room and looking out of the window, I noticed that the road which was normally empty had many people, mainly women, standing around, some of them crying. I could not understand why, but I was soon to find out that just after nine o'clock on that 21st October (Friday morning), in 1966, 144 people, 116 of them children, were killed when a coal tip slid onto a primary school and houses close by, in the village of Aberfan, near the town of Merthyr Tydfil - a bus ride away.

There is no need for me to go into the detail of what took place that day, for if you are interested in finding out, you can do the research for yourself; but years later I visited the site where a garden had been made in memory of that tragic day in 1966 - a day, even all these years later, as I remember, my heart feels heavy.

Time is moving on and my daughter is 7 years of age, and there is another surprise: I am pregnant again, and when the baby is born, it is another little boy who weighs in at 8 pound. I don't go into hospital this time, but give birth to him at home, and he too has all his fingers and toes.

Now we have four children, three boys and a girl, but how can I remember all the things we did together while living in this house? There were so many memories, like the times we walked to the top of the mountain at the back of the house, carrying lemonade and sandwiches, just waiting to be eaten when we reached the top. Then how we would look down on all the cars that looked like tiny ants running along the road and try and guess who was in them and where they were going; the times when, with my friend and her children, we would walk down the hill and cross the main road to fields where blackberry bushes grew alongside, and gather blackberries to make a blackberry pie, and I say to the children "don't eat all the blackberry's or there will not be enough to make a pie" as they look at me and smile with dyed blue lips, and as I write I think to myself, I have been down this road before.

The steelworks near Swansea is the next place I remember him working. The steelworks (pronounced Felindre in Welsh, or Velindre in English), produced millions of tons of tin plate. It was first opened in 1956, but later shut down in 1989. Swansea is a town along the coast of South Wales, and again is full of history. It was first founded by the Normans who conquered the area in the 12th century and later became part of the industrial revolution, with copper being smelted. Several docks were built which helped their shipping, and the building of ships and some of the many famous people who were born not far away from Swansea were Richard Burton, a famous Welsh actor, and Sir Anthony Hopkins, who still today we see in our cinemas.

Again, for a time, all seemed to be going well - the children were happy, healthy and growing up; he had regular work, and I enjoyed looking after my home, which we had now been in for a few years. It was then we were told of a new housing estate that was being built not far from the one we were living in where, because there was a large communal boiler, when you turned on the central heating, your house could be heated without first making a fire, and the heating would be included in the rent; because coal was getting more expensive to buy, we decided that while he had a regular job with a good wage, we would apply to the council to move.

So move we did to a new house, where downstairs there was a large sitting room and a dining room, with a back door that opened onto a balcony; a small kitchen and toilet at the front of the house, then three bedrooms and a bathroom upstairs. Built underneath the back of the house was a garage, but of course at this time neither of us could drive. The good thing about this house was that the front door did not open onto a road, so I was never worried when the children were playing outside, as long as they kept to the front of the house (which was the first rule laid down).

It was about this time, while he had a regular job, that we decided it would be a good thing for him to get a driving license, as having a car would mean getting around would be easier, and instead of taking a bus each day to work, a car would cut quite a bit of time off his work day. So the second-hand car that we bought was a Riley Saloon. I remember it was very square, and the colour, I think, was dark green; more than that I cannot remember, but once he passed the government driving test we began to visit the different seaside towns that were not too far away, such as Porth Call and Barry Island. We would also drive to the Brecon Beacons, where we would enjoy, on sunny days, walking alongside the many little streams, where the children would take off their shoes and socks and paddle in the water, and later drink the lemonade and eat the sandwiches that we had taken for a picnic. The Brecon Beacons are a range of mountains not far from Aberdare and are named after an old tradition of lighting fires as beacons to warn of attacks by the English when they were at war, centuries earlier, with the people of Wales.

Time continues to move on, and even my youngest son is in school; it seems funny not having any children around during the day - what shall I do with myself, I ask. At first the days seem long, as I am not used to being on my own, but once the housework is done, I do secretly enjoy the time that becomes mine - but there is always some thing waiting around the next bend in the road, and what was waiting for me was something that I least expected.

The children were home after their school day. I was cooking tea ready for when he arrived home from work, and because he now drove, he was always home with in an expected time. I look at the clock thinking 'he will be home soon,' knowing the food will be ready on time, but the hands of the clock are moving on, and he has not arrived. He must be held up in traffic, I am thinking as the hands on the clock are still moving, but now I am thinking the food will be over cooked if he does not arrive soon. 'You had better come and have your tea now' I say to the children; Dad must be held up in traffic. They sit down at the table 'you get on and eat' I say, all the time looking at the clock and waiting for the sound of the key in the door, but the hands of the clock keep moving, and now I am beginning to worry; I have never known him to be so late. The tea is finished and I have washed up, but he is still not home. What shall I do? I can't worry the children, but already they can sense the fear in me, and now they begin to give all the reasons they think why he is late. He's in a traffic jam, he's got a puncture, he's given a lift home to someone at work; but I am beginning to sense the fear in their minds now, so I try to stay calm for there sake, so say 'that must be it.'

It is now late evening; soon it will be dark, and he is still not home. Something must have happened; he must have been in an accident I say to myself, but I can no longer just sit and wait, so I decide we should go to my sister's house. I leave a note telling him where we are, asking him to come and pick us up as soon as he gets home. I bet just as we get to your aunt's he will be there waiting for us, I say, hoping what I have said will be true, but when we arrive the car is not there, and now I am telling my sister and brother-in-law of the situation, and again all reasons are given why he could be late, but deep down I know that something is wrong. I stay for a while; we are all making small talk, but I know we are all thinking the same thing and, after finishing a cup of tea that has been made, I say I think I ought to go home now. Because my brother-in-law has a car, we all pile in and begin our journey home, but what is that I see behind us? It's an ambulance and it's following us around the housing estate. Pull over I say, let it over, take us, and now we are following it, but it doesn't turn off into another road, it is stopping outside our house.

I don't remember getting out of the car, all I remember is watching the doors of the ambulance opening and him being helped out. Are you alright, I say (what a stupid question). I'm alright he says, as he hobbles to the front door. Once inside, he tells of the car that, coming in the opposite direction, rears across the road and hits our car head on. The car is a write-off he says, but I have the green shield stamps. What do you mean? I ask. Well, he says, when I got out of the car and was being helped into the ambulance all I could think of was my green shield stamps, so back to the car I went and got them from the glove compartment. What about your tools that are in the boot I say. Oh, I never thought about them till after, he says, but I will pick them up later.

Green Shield Stamps were part of a shop loyalty scheme, and for every 6 old pennies (or 2 ½ pence), you spent in a shop, they would give you one stamp, then you would stick this into a small book till the book was full; then you would exchange these for gifts that you chose from a catalogue, but sometimes you could tear out just the amount of full pages for a gift that was less than the hole book. Of course not all shops did this, but you would normally buy from the shop that did, so you could quickly fill the book. Today these stamps have been replaced by store loyalty cards.

As he told me the story of what had happened, I could not believe that the green shields stamps were what he had returned to the car for before getting into the ambulance. Thinking about the expensive tools which he would always need for his work would have seemed

159

more logical, but later we laughed about this, not just then but for many years later; we always said it was the bump on the head that made him not quite right that day.

It was several weeks before he was able to return to work, as it was not only the bump on the head that he had received, but also other minor injuries, but at least he was all in one piece and we had him safely home - more than could be said about the car.

They say that all good things must come to an end, and to an end they came, for it was not long before once again he found himself out of work by being made redundant, and the issue of money once more reared its ugly head. I remember the times when I would hide on the stairs with the children, telling them to be quiet when the milkman knocked for his money; the times when, again, the gas and electric bills dropped on the mat and because they could not be paid, I would have to phone the companies and ask them to give me time to pay. Everything, it seemed, was going from bad to worse again, so I knew the only solution was for me to go back to work.

Now I found myself working in an open-fronted wet fish shop owned by a man and his wife. I worked full time Monday to Saturday, with a half day on Wednesday. Fridays were especially busy, as Friday was known as fish day, and it was not long before I began to get home each day smelling more and more like a fish; the children, as I walked through the door, would often pinch their noses and say 'Oh Mum you smell of fish.'

It was not long before the customers began to get used to me, and soon they were telling me about the things that were going on in their lives, and then they were talking to me, using my name, but the customer I remember most is the man who owned a fish and chip shop who regularly bought his fish from us. I remember how, once a week, he would buy a large place (the name of a fish) for him and his wife, and as I weighed and filleted the fish for him he would stand

and talk, telling me about his family and his business. It was not long before that he asked if I would go and work for him, but even though working in his shop would have been warmer, it meant that I would have to work evenings, and that was not something I wanted to do at this time.

As I am writing about the time I worked there I remember how, during cold days, the only heat we had was from a little electric fire that was in the small office at the back of the shop, but of course I had to be in the front most of the time, and with the shop being all open with a fish slab that had to be kept cold, and fish sometimes being taken from boxes filled with ice, my hands and body never seemed to get warm. I remember one time when my aunt (the one who plaited her hair so fast) came with her husband to see me in the shop, they could not understand why I would work in such conditions, and even to this day she often speaks about the time she remembers me working there, and it still upsets her, but now I must go back just a little way in time.

My Mum and Dad were still living in Ealing, but because of a change in their circumstances, they decided that they wanted to move to Wales to be near my sister and me. We were both a bit concerned about this… moving away from an area that had been their home for so many years and also leaving their friends. We felt that if it did not work out for them, they would become unhappy and regret moving, so even though it was something my sister and I wanted, we left the decision to them.

But move they did, to an area called Godreaman, which is a small mining village not far from Aberdare. I was very excited at the thought of them living just across the valley, as this would mean I would be close to them once more. We had managed to find a terrace house for them to rent, and even though the rooms needed decorating, we all joined in with this task. Once all their furniture was arranged they soon settled down, even planting flowers and vegetables in the

161

garden at the back of the house - something that they had never been able to do. The joy on their faces when, each time they showed me around the garden, pointing out all that was growing "look at the size of those runner beans" I hear Dad say; "I cant believe how many are growing on one plant; we wont need to buy any at all this year." As I am writing this, I can see him with a smile on his face, looking through the thick growth of leaves and almost counting each bean, but it's my turn to smile now as I remember.

Now to continue:-

Having a car had made such a lot of difference to us, and now because we no longer had one our trips to the seaside had ceased. Then one Saturday afternoon on a visit to another friend he told us of a car that he knew of that had been parked outside a house for months, and that maybe the person who owned it might just want to get rid of it. We explained that there was no way we had money for a car, but he insisted that it should be looked at, so before I had a chance to say anything else they had both gone.

Now I am waiting and wondering; what were we thinking? There was no way we could afford a car. How much would the man want for it? Secretly I am hoping that he would say that he did not want to sell it.

It was not long before I heard the sound of an engine, and soon we were all running to the door – me, my children, my friend and her children, and as I look back, we must have looked a funny site, all walking round and round the car that stood in front of us.

But what a car it turned out to be! A 'Ford Consul Mark 1', which was first built in the early 1950s, and sounds so glamorous, but there was nothing glamorous about the car that stood in front of me. The only thing that was holding this car together was the dirt and grease on the bodywork, and when I opened the door he was sitting there with a grin on his face, as if he had just purchased a Rolls Royce; but there was worse to come, for when he got out of the car and I looked inside, the first thing I noticed was that the front bench seat was torn in several places; then, as I looked at the floor, it was covered in rubbish, and the smell was awful. All that was bad enough: till he got back in the car and then turned on the engine, within minutes smoke was pouring out of the exhaust pipe. My first words were 'how much does he want for it.' His answer came back 'ten Pounds,' and said that he had already paid him, so there was no taking it back.

Don't worry about the engine, the friend said, we can get a second-hand one from the scrap yard, and I will put it in for you. So without waiting for any reply, the car was started and they were gone, with black smoke following them. First stop the scrap yard. Now I know what you're thinking and saying to yourself "what did she expect for ten pounds?" But ten pounds was worth more then it is today, and a lot more when what you spend it on is not worth a penny of it!

It was a few days later that work on the car began, and after a lot of huffing and puffing a second hand engine had been installed. Once all the nuts and bolts had been tightened and everything was in place, the next thing was to turn the key. I didn't wait around to find out if the engine would start, as my heart was in my mouth, hoping it would start, and at the same time, afraid it would blow up in front of me, so I took the coward's way out and went back into the house and stood there, with my hands over my ears and thinking 'I hope they remembered to put oil in the engine.'

Soon I heard the engine roaring away. I couldn't believe it had started first time! I ran down to the garage and they were standing there, covered in oil and grease, with a look of satisfaction on their faces that said "We did it."

Now that the engine was in place, it was the body work that needed attention, so the first job was to give the car a good wash inside and out. First we cleaned the inside, taking out all the rubbish that had

163

been thrown in there. There were screws, bolts, engine parts, empty crisp packets, cigarette butts, dead matches and even a few coins, but even after all the cleaning, the front seat was still ripped, and the body work looked rough.

Two journeys were made, the first to the scrap yard where we managed to buy a second-hand bench seat ,and then to Woolworth's (a shop that had been going for nearly a hundred years, and is known affectingly as Woollies), which sold almost everything, but that day we bought just a tin of cream coloured gloss paint. Sadly, these shops have now all been closed.

Soon, with brushes in hand, we started painting away, and when the first coat of paint was dry we started all over again, and when that was finished we stood back and looked at the car with pride and we both said "who would have thought that this car could have looked so good". No longer was it dirt and grease holding everything together; now it was paint that covered a multitude of sins, and we couldn't wait for the paint to dry quickly enough so the car could be let loose onto the road. Can't we try it now, the boys say? No the paint's not dry yet, he says, but really he can't wait either. Soon the paint does dry, and we are all inside and cautiously being driven onto the road. 'Everything seems fine,' he says, above all the chatter and giggles in the car from the excitement that we all felt; and everything **was** fine, for the car ran smoothly, cruising along the road. Once again, I am going to tell you a story that, at the time was quite frightening, but when we looked back over the years, it was a story that not only made us laugh, but whoever we told it too.

We had wanted to take the children on a holiday for a few days, and the easiest way for us to do this was to go camping, as all we would have to pay for was for pitching the tent in a field and the petrol to get there and food we would have had to buy anyway. So camping it was, but the problem was, we didn't have a tent, so after speaking to my friend who said that they would like to come too, they said that they knew someone who would be willing to lend us one.

Now all talk was of spending a few days camping, and as the time to leave was drawing nearer, the children were getting more and more excited, till finally the day arrived and, after packing the car with everything except the kitchen sink, we were ready to drive to the camp site, the name of which I cannot remember but I do know that it was located West of London.

As we travelled down the motorway, the weather was hot and sunny; the children were excited, especially the two older boys, who were looking forward to spending their nights in a small tent that we had bought for them to sleep in. All they talked about was sleeping in the tent outside in an open field, and their Dad, well he was just as excited as they were. As for me, all I can say is that I was doing this for the children; but the car did us proud, for we arrived safely (but I must confess that all the time, at the back of my mind, was the thought 'its going to break down any minute').

We filled our days doing all the things you do on a camping holiday. We played cricket and rounders on the field, met other campers who also joined in the games; we sunbathed, read books and just enjoyed each day being together as a family. I even managed to cook on the small camping stove that we had brought with us. Every thing was going well, that is till the Saturday night before we were due to go home on the Sunday. We had decided to leave as late as possible before dismantling the tent on the Sunday, as the children were enjoying themselves so much, but during Saturday night we were woken up by the sound of wind and rain. It was no light shower, for it sounded as if the heavens had opened, and all the rain was directed at us. As I lay there, I expected that any minute the wind would tear the tent pegs from the ground, sending the tent flying through the air. "I think I ought to go and check the boys" he says, and I thought 'rather you than me,' as he opened the door of the tent and went out. Are they ok, I ask when he comes back, wet and shivering; they're fine, he says, they are both fast asleep. Has the rain got in their tent I ask? No, he says, they're fine.

Morning finally came, but the rain was still pouring down, so we decided that we would pack up and leave for home as soon as possible, but dismantling the tent was not so easy, as it was now soaking wet, and when we tried to roll it to put it in its cover it just would not go in. The only thing we could do was to fold it, but even when we did that, we could still not even fit it in the boot of the car, so we ended up having to put it on the back seat, but this meant that there was no way we could get all the children in the car. My friends said that they would take one of the boys and my daughter with them, which left my oldest son on the back seat, squeezed between the tent and the door, and my other son sitting on my lap; but we still had all the clothes and equipment we had taken with us, so we put as much as we could in the boot of the car and just filled every space that we could find around us.

He is soon assuring all of us that we would soon be home, as it would not take too long; being Sunday, there would not be a lot of traffic on the road. What he had not planned for was the next situation, for we were not a mile down the road before the windscreen wiper on his side of the car decided not to work. He pulled over, got out of the car, and did his best trying to fix it, but no matter how hard he tried, it would not work. 'Can't we buy a new windscreen wiper' I say; it's not the wiper, he says, it's the whole thing that's not working. What are we going to do now I say? I'll just have to look out your side of the windscreen. So, getting back in the car, the first thing he says is that we cannot go on the motorway home, as that would be too dangerous; it would have to be across country. This would take us much longer but would be safer.

This was the one time that I was glad that we had a front bench seat in the car, as he was able to slide across and look out of my side of the windscreen, and because it was a column gear change instead of the gears being on the floor of the car, it is attached to the steering column; this made it easer to drive. I'm sure this will be OK, I say to myself, but all the time feeling very nervous. I'm sure it will be OK, but we had not gone far when the windscreen wiper my side of the car began to slow down, for when the wiper hit the bottom of the windscreen, it decided that it did not want to come back up. Once again he stops the car, gets out and tries to mend it, and once again he gets back in and says there is nothing he can do. 'I know,' I say, as I start hunting for a towel. I'll rap this around my hand and with the window down put my hand out and every time the wiper comes down it will hit my hand and go back up again. You can't do that, he says, you'll freeze; but that is what I did, and because we had to travel the long way home, it took us about seven hours. It never stopped raining once, but we did get home safely, and I had a steaming hot bath once I got home, while he took care of the children and emptied the car.

That was another story we often spoke and laughed about over the years, even though it was not funny at the time.

Once again time has moved on, and the road I am travelling is seeing the children growing up and each of them growing into people that I am proud of. The oldest has left school now, and the second will not be far behind. There is still no regular work for him, but he is not the only one who is finding it hard to find work, as many of the coal mines are being closed and men who have worked for many years underground can no longer find regular employment. He has tried several times to start his own business, and he did manage to get a few small jobs, but never enough to support the family, so I continued to work. I am no longer at the fish shop, because the long hours during the week that I had to work, besides all day Saturday, I felt was no longer good for the family, so we agreed that I should look for some thing with fewer hours.

The next job I found was working as a receptionist in a hotel, which I cannot remember the name of, and even if you were to ask me now where about it was in Aberdare, I cannot remember that either. I only know that I had to rely on him to take me to work each day in the car and pick me up at the end of the different shifts that I had to work. I did think when I took the job that doing the shift work would suit me better, but doing this did not turn out as I had expected, as we had decided to move again to a house that was cheaper to rent, this time in a village called Penrhiwceiber (or Kyber, for short), near the town of Mountain Ash. First let me tell you something about the village of Penrhiwceiber and the town of Mountain Ash.

Part 13.

PENRHIWCEIBER

Even though the village of Penrhiwceiber is not very big, there is much history to be found for those who want to delve into it's past. At one time there was a colliery known as Penrikyer Colliery, which was opened in 1872 and closed in 1985, and for those who laid down there lives during three wars (World War I, then World War II, and then the Korean War), there is a memorial clock tower that had been erected in remembrance of them in the village. It also boasts of a Workmen's Hall, which was opened in 1888 and restored 1992. There are rows and rows of houses built on the side of a mountain, with many roads that look so steep you wonder if you will ever get to the top, with some having handrails (which I was glad of many a time). Then there is Mountain Ash, a small town with one main street running through it with shops on either side. It has a very striking building which is used as its town hall (which I will tell you about a little later). Once a year, the famous 'Nos Galan' races are run there, which is Welsh for New Year's Eve. These races began in 1958, and have had many famous runners join in the fun of the events, one being Linford Christie, a hundred-meter Olympic sprinter. The races are in memory of a Welsh athlete, Guto Nyth Bran, a legendry athlete whose statue is situated in the town, but there is so much fascinating history about this man, I am sure you would enjoy spending some time reading all about them for yourselves.

Now I must tell you about the house that we lived in.

The house was one of many terrace houses built on the side of a mountain. To reach it, you first had to walk up one of the roads that you never felt that you would ever reach the top of before having a heart attack, but fortunately, because it had a rail to help with the climb, you would eventually get there.

I remember that there were steps which took you up even higher, leading to the front door, which opened onto a long passage, and as you looked to your right there were two doors - the first opened onto a room which I would call the front room. Once inside this room, to the right was a bay window, and when looking through this you would see a very small front garden. The second door opened onto a sitting room, and once inside this room, to your left there was another door which led to the kitchen. I remember that in this room on the far wall stood a Rayburn stove, which in a way reminded me of the stove that was in the house that he grew up in. Then there was another door, at the side of the same wall that the stove was on, leading to a very small bathroom but as you walked into the kitchen there was also a door to the right that led to a small outhouse where the cooker and a few cupboards were built. There was another door at the end of this that led to a garden that was so steep we never once used it. I remember how pleased I was when I saw the Rayburn range, as I knew that I was able to burn almost anything in this fire besides using the oven that was built alongside it. I remember how many a times I would make a broth and put it in the oven at night, and by the morning, it would be cooked; because the fire stayed alight all night, in the morning, coming downstairs you knew that when you opened the kitchen door you would be greeted with warm air, and sometimes the smell of cooking.

Upstairs there were four bedrooms, but I cannot describe these, as I find it hard to remember exactly what they looked like, and again as I write I ask myself why I do not remember some things, when other things stand out so clearly about this house. I think maybe it's because I was never happy while living there, even though we did try to make it 'home.' On one occasion, we decided to knock down the dividing wall between the two rooms downstairs to make a much larger room, as we never seemed to use the front room, but even doing this did not make living there any easier.

The time has moved on and the three oldest are all now working, and

I am no longer having to travel to the hotel, but have found temporary work in a cooked chicken factory. I remember having to get up really early for a morning shift, and he has a job there as a van driver delivering the cooked chicken to various businesses but again it is not long before we are <u>both</u> unemployed this time.

It was while we were living here that once again I found myself pregnant, but this time it was more of a surprise than ever, as my youngest son was now 10 years old, and I had never dreamed that I would have another child; but soon I was holding another son in my arms. My family now consisted of four boys and one girl, but no matter how hard I tried, for some reason I still could not settle into this house and became very unhappy, until one day my oldest son came home and said that while he had been in Aberdare, he had met a friend of ours who had told him that she and her family had moved to the new town of Milton Keynes in Buckinghamshire, and because of the large town that was being built, tradesmen were being encouraged to move there and of course with this would come accommodation.

A new town, a new job, a new house; hadn't I been down this road before? Could I face being turned down again if, for some reason, we were not accepted as the same procedure would have to be gone through. It all sounded so good, but this time the children were not babies, so their futures had to be taken into consideration. Would the move be right not just for him and me, but for them as well? They were all working; would they be willing to give up their jobs and take the chance of moving, hoping that they would be able to find work in this new town?

After discussing it with them, it was decided that he would go to the local job centre and ask if they could find out if there were any vacancies for plumbers in Milton Keynes, and then we would make any decisions after that, but when he came back home, he said that there was another town that was looking for workers and that was Thetford in Norfolk. So it was decided that whatever vacancy came up first, we would go there.

So began a different topic of conversation that night, and we were all excited at the thought that soon we could be moving to a new house, and there would be a different future for us all; but we certainly did not expect that the future would change so quickly, for the following day he received a telegram from the Job Centre telling him that an appointment had been made for him to attend that day.

Can you imagine the excitement that we both felt? We never dreamed that he would hear from them so soon; it was not long before, all smartly dressed, he left for the appointment.

Even though I had plenty to occupy myself with, what with the new baby and trying to do things in the house, all the time my mind was wondering what was happening in the Job Centre, and though I tried not to build my hopes up too much, I still could not wait for him to come home and I knew that I would just have to look at him to know whether it was good news or bad.

Once again the hands on the clock seemed never to move, as he seemed to have been gone for such a long time, and then I heard the key in the door, and I knew when I saw him that his news was going to be good.

I have an interview with a plumbing and heating firm in Milton Keynes, he says. I have spoken to the owner over the phone and have made arrangements to go there to see him.

There is no way I can tell you how excited I was now; I was looking forward for the children to come home from work to tell them the news that just *maybe* we would be moving.

A few days later he left for Milton Keynes, taking my older son with him, and once again all I do is watch the clock, but this time I know that they will be gone all day, for Milton Keynes is near London, so it would not be till late that night that they would be home. I try to keep busy once again, still with one eye on the clock, but there is no going to bed before they're home and watching the television is just a noise in the back of my mind, for I cannot concentrate on anything, and then the key in the door is turned, and as they walk through the door, the look is tired but happy.

I got the job he says, and I start work next week, and although I am glad, I ask the question 'where are you going to live?' I will have to find a room till we get the house, he says. I have been given a form to give to our local Council; you must take that in as soon as possible, as they have to give the OK, the sooner we will have the house. Now I am not thinking of his job or his finding a room, or even being on my own with out him; for a while all I can think of is the visit to the Town Hall, filling in forms and the person who will come and interview us and I wonder if the answer will be any different this time.

What happens if they turn us down I say; they won't do that, he says, but I don't have the faith he does and even though plans are made for him to leave, I still cannot get out of my mind the time that we were turned down for a new town, years earlier.

Soon he would be leaving to start his new job and when we told the friend who had first told us about Milton Keynes that he had managed to find work and was moving there, she said that she knew a family who would give him accommodation, and because they were friends of hers, this made us feel a lot happier.

The day arrived for him to leave, and it was not easy watching him go. Because there was so much for me to have to sort out while he was away, I wondered how I was going to do it all, but at least I would not have to do it on my own, as having a grown up family they would help with all the packing - but wait a minute, I have not taken the form to the Council Office yet! I do not know if they will approve the move.

First thing Monday morning I make my way to the Town Hall in Mountain Ash to hand in the form from his new employer, explaining about the move, and even though this building, first built in 1904 is splendid to look at, it has for me a feeling of apprehension. Soon I am being asked questions and watch, as all that I say is being written down in front of me. Someone will soon be out to visit you, I am told; then asked 'have you any questions?' But the question I want to ask I don't say out loud: I just want to know why you can't just say yes now? I want to shout out loud, but instead I say 'no thank you' and smile as I get up from the chair and leave the room, closing the door behind me.

Each weekend for the next two weeks he comes home, but then says it is costing too much money in petrol so he won't be home the following weekend, and because I have not had the visit that I am not looking forward to, and because we are still not sure of what is going to happen, none of the children can give notice to leave their jobs. At last there is a knock at the door, and standing there is the man who has our future in his hands, but this time after he leaves there is no feeling that it all went wrong, and no wishing that I could answer his questions all over again. This time I just knew that every thing was going to be alright, and so it was.

Part 14.

MILTON KEYNES

Milton Keynes, a new town that has grown in size and population since our arrival here 30 years ago, and as I write, I ask myself: do I have any regrets about the decision we made in moving to this part of the country - and the answer has to be no.

Milton Keynes is situated about 53 miles from London and was built in the area of Buckinghamshire. It takes in towns such as Bletchley, Wolverton, Stony Stratford, Newport Pagnell, and many other local villages. Again, this part of the country is steeped in English history, dating back many hundreds of years. Many stories are told, from the several inns were built here, especially in the town of Stony Stratford. So again, I encourage you to spend a little time reading about those fascinating times and learning about the people who once lived in this area and those who visited.

Milton Keynes (some times given the title "City") boasts of the millions of trees that have been planted, and because of this we have become known as the City of Trees. It has many miles of paths for cyclists and pedestrians; parks that are part of the open land space, and the tranquillity of Grand Union Canal, which winds through the towns branching from the River Thames at Brentford, West of London, and ends in Birmingham, a city that lies North in the U.K.

The canal is about one 137 miles long and, by the way, is only a few hundred yards from where I live. At one time it was used to transport merchandise, but of course this is no longer necessary, so today it is used only by people who live on long-boats, holiday makers, and of course, fishermen. We also have one of the largest covered shopping centres in Europe, so whether the sun shines or the rain pours, it is always a good day to shop!!! I have always felt that the only thing that seems to be missing from this area is the sea; but for me this was another journey, and as I stood in front of the house that I was to live in, I could never have guessed that the road I was about to travel would alter my life so dramatically. Before you take that journey with me, let me describe to you the house that has become such a part of my memories.

The first thing I noticed as we drove towards the house was the avenue of trees, and even though they were still young, the picture they painted was one of calm; even now, 30 years later, when looking out of my window and see how tall and majestic they have grown, I never tire of watching how their leaves seem to dance in the wind. In autumn, they turn to all the rustic colours you can imagine, and even in winter, though the leaves have dropped, they become dressed in white from the frost that visits.

As the van (the one that he was given by his employer) pulled up outside the house, I noticed the long path that leads to the front door - this was about 25 feet long (7.62 meters), and on either side of this there were lawns, but only on one side is the lawn the length of the path, as the other side has a car port taking up some of the area. It suddenly occurred to me that this was the first time that I had such a large front garden, and my only thought now was what was waiting for me when I open the front door.

The door opened onto a small passage where there was a door to the right, which I soon realised was a toilet. Then, facing me, was another door which opened onto an open plan area with two doors to the left, the first being a downstairs bedroom, the second a walk-in cupboard. In front of me was another door which opened on to a sitting room which is the width of the house (this is about 30 feet wide, or 9 meters). Once inside the sitting room, I noticed that it was divided by stairs taking you up to a bathroom and three bedrooms. There were another two doors in this room; one opened to a 50 foot (15.24 meters), garden, which again, was all lawn with two small trees planted at the bottom - one a sycamore, the other an apple tree, which we were to discover would grow Granny Smith cooking apples. Then the door at the end of the room leads us back to the front of the house, where a reasonable-sized kitchen looked all pink.

When I first stepped in side I noticed how the people who had lived there before us must have liked the colours pink and dark brown, as most of the bedrooms were of this dark shade. The kitchen they had painted pink, and in the sitting room, wide brown stripes had be painted all around the walls - but I looked beyond all the colours and stripes - all I could see was how the rooms would look in the future when the dark colours and the pink had gone, and I thought to myself that living in this house was going to be the best time of all.

So we began to settle in. It was not long before the three older children were all employed, and with my younger son settled into school, I spent my days at home with the baby and getting to know my way around the area. Because the shopping centre had not yet been opened, it was to Wolverton or Bletchley I would have to travel for my main shopping. I soon learnt that Bletchley was a town where, during the war, a large house known as "Bletchley Park" had been used as a code-breaking centre, and the famous German Enigma code had been cracked by the men and women who worked there; Wolverton was where a new royal train had been built in 1903.

Why I started work once again I cannot remember. Whether it was a shortage of money or for any other reason I do not know, but I found myself working as a domestic cleaner at Renny Lodge Hospital in Newport Pagnell, but this time doing only part time hours as my youngest son was still only a baby. I worked from 5:00PM till 8:00PM every Monday, Wednesday and Friday; and from 8:00PM till 12:00AM, and 5:00PM till 8:00PM Saturday and Sunday. I was able to do the evening hours as my daughter, who was the only one who finished her working day in time, made it possible for me to start my shift at 5:00 o'clock, taking care of the baby 'til he came home from work. I remember in the beginning how, because it was difficult to get a bus to get me to work on time, I borrowed a bicycle from a friend, and so would cycle to work; but I soon realised that getting there was much easier than coming home, as the roads seem to slant down going, but coming home the roads seemed to grow higher as I had to push harder on the pedals (or maybe at the end of the shift it just seemed harder). Then my daughter decided that she would buy herself a 49 c.c. motor scooter and guess what? I learnt to ride it; soon the roads getting higher did not bother me any more.

Now let me tell you a little about Renny Lodge and Newport Pagnell.

Renny Lodge was first built in 1836 as a workhouse, but because in 1929 work houses were abolished, it then became a hospital, caring for the elderly. It closed in 1992 and was demolished in 1994 to make way for housing, but long before this building was erected, Newport Pagnell was a pre-iron age settlement, and was first mentioned in the Doomsday Book of 1086. Even today, the history of many of the buildings go back hundreds of years, some of these include churches, a hotel that was once a coaching inn, and even a cast iron bridge called Tickford Bridge, which was built in 1810 and is still being used today. I think the name that will stand out most to you will be Aston Martin, because it is here, on Tickford Street, Newport Pagnell, that the building of these cars took place in the 1950s, but once again this has all stopped, as the factory was closed and sold in 2007. Here I must confess that much of the fascinating history that I have learnt about the many places that I have lived has only come about because of this writing, but you don't have to wait as long as I have before you can learn about your surroundings; because of the internet, all information is now at your fingertips, and you will be surprised, as I have, to how much history surrounds the places we live; and even now I say to myself "I lived there and I never knew that."

One of the reasons I think I settled so quickly in Milton Keynes was that as soon as we told my Mum and Dad that we were moving nearer to London strait away with out even thinking about it they said that they wanted to move with us which told me that moving and leaving London as they had done had not been the right thing for them and so began a series of phone calls to the Council offices and because houses were far easier to come by as the town was being built and people were being encourage to move here they were soon given a bungalow on a housing estate called Stacy Bushes which they accepted with out even looking at it first.

When the furniture van arrived, with their home piled high inside and them in the car following, I was full of apprehension. I kept thinking 'would they like their new home, or would they regret accepting something that they had never seen,' but I need not have worried, for from the moment they saw the bungalow, without even having stepped inside, I could tell from their faces and all the encouraging sounds (such as 'ooh' and 'aah'), that they felt that they had made the right decision about moving, but how they felt about leaving my sister, who had settled well in Aberdare, or how my sister felt about them leaving, I don't think I ever really found out. I only know that they loved the bungalow and the life that went with it, and now because the journey travelling back to Ealing to see there friends and family was only an hour away, this seamed to give both of them a new lease on life. They often travelled to Greenford, west London, to see my aunt (the one who had platted her hair so fast and who they had stayed very close to over the years). Sadly my aunt's first marriage had not lasted, but a few years later she met and married another man who she loved passionately, and who loved her in return and was now living in Greenford west of London. This was an easy journey for my Mum and Dad to make, so trips to London became part of their life - that was a happy one - and me? Well, I sighed with relief, for if they were happy, so was I.

Time is moving on, and the three oldest children have all settled down to married life; the baby is no longer a baby, but has started school and has settled well. I am still working in Renny Lodge and still enjoying the time I spend there; and for him there has been the sadness of both his parents dying and several different jobs that have come and gone. Now, as I write, I am searching my memory to try and remember many of the things that must have happened during those years, but all there is are the weddings, and the joy they bought at that time; my youngest son starting school, which he enjoyed from day one. Why is this, I am asking myself as I write - why can't I remember more of the things that must of happened day by day, but there is no answer and no memory, that is until the first heartbreaking event for me takes place - the death of my Dad.

There had been no indication that he was seriously ill, as almost to the end he was going out most days, catching a bus to Wolverton with Mum to do their shopping, and still enjoying time in their small garden. He no longer drove a car, as, on a visit to my Mum and Dad, my sister and brother-in-law had decided that it was not safe for him to drive, so had convinced my Dad to sell the car, while Mum was out with me: much to the anger of Mum when she arrived home and found out what they had done without first discussing it with her.

I remember his not being well seemed to start after they had been on holiday with us. We had decided to have a week's holiday at Butlins, in the seaside town of Bognor Regis in West Sussex, which is on the south coast. This town was originally named Bognor but was changed after King George V convalesced there in 1929.

I remember that, even though it was the summertime, the weather was wet and cold and no matter what Dad wore, he was never able to get warm. After the holiday it was not surprising that he caught a cold, but this time instead of him not being well just for a week or two even, after the cold had gone he still was not right. So a visit to the doctor was insisted on by Mum, and soon after an X-ray at the hospital revealed that he had lung cancer. How can I describe the devastation of hearing those words, as even now I am finding it hard just to write them down? Did any of us really understand what all this meant? I am not sure we did. The only one who had been close to me who had died of this terrible disease had been my Nan, but because I was no longer living in London at the time of her death, I did not know much about it.

It was not long after learning of his illness that he seemed to deteriorate, so a stay in hospital was recommended by his doctor, but Dad was not happy about this as he had never been in hospital since being a young man, but Mum advised him that he should go. He was not there long, as on a visit with her to see him as he sat at a table having his tea and trying to eat an ice cream I noticed he was unable to cut into it, and I was wondering why, then soon realised that his eyesight had deteriorated so badly that he could not see that the ice cream still had its paper wrapping on it. It was then that both Mum and I decided that he must come home, as he was getting no more from the hospital than we could do for him at home. So home he came, and I am sure that each day that Mum and Dad spent together was a time treasured by both. My time too had changed, as I was spending as much of it as I could with them, but never taking any time away from them wanting to be on there own, until one evening Mum was so down that she asked me to stay the night, which I did, but during that evening I am sure that Dad knew that it was time for him to say goodbye, as just listening to the things that he was saying I felt he knew. Then, falling asleep, he passed away the next day.

Now the road I am taking has a sharp bend, and while I am travelling on this part of the road, it is the hardest one that I have faced up till now, as like most of us, we believe that our parents (even though they are much older) will all ways be with us and so never think of the day we may lose them.

I spent as much time as I could, helping my Mum with her grieving. There were days when she would smile, but something about that smile told be me it was not real, and as the days turned into months, there was little change. I would encourage her to visit my sister and my aunt in Greenford, hoping that the time away would help, but it never did. It was not long before she too became ill with cancer, and just two years after the death of my Dad, I lost my Mum.

I cannot explain to you how I felt, but up until that time all I can say is that nothing I had experienced before came close to what I felt then, and writing this all down has brought back memories and feelings that I had thought I had forgotten, which tells me that we don't ever really forget, we just tuck the memory away. (Time once again to put the kettle on).

Several months before Mum died, I had come to the conclusion that riding the scooter in all sorts of weather was becoming too much for me, and so I decided that I would learn to drive a car. Taking driving lessons was a new experience, and after the third attempt at a driving test, I was finally allowed to drive on the road on my own. One of the biggest regrets that I have is that Mum died without her even getting into the car with me, as I did not pass the test till just before she died. When I think of all the places I could have taken her, and all the fun we could have had, it makes me sad even now.

Now that three of the children had married and left home, I realised that no longer could I work evenings during the week, as I could not always rely on him being home in time to look after the younger ones. I was just about to ask my employer if I could change my hours from working evenings, when I was told that the domestic part of the hospital was going to be handed over to a private firm, and after an interview a few weeks later with one of there personnel officers, I knew there was no way I could work the hours they offered, and so took redundancy.

The day I left Renny Lodge was a sad day, as I had enjoyed working there, but now I had to find another job and knew that this was not going to be easy, as the only experience I'd had over the last few years was that of a domestic cleaner. I knew I wanted to do something different, but what? So a trip to the job centre was my next stop.

'*Wanted: A Care Assistant for Private Residential Care Home*', I read on the notice board. I think I will try for that, I say to myself, but as I read further down it says 'night shifts'. So now I am asking myself 'could I work nights?' but then I am thinking nights would suit me fine, as no longer would I have to worry about him being home in time to look after the children, as I would not have to start my shifts till late. Within minutes I am on the phone making an appointment with the owner of the care home, and soon I am driving to the town of Olney and after an interview, I have been accepted for the job.

Olney: where every year on Shrove Tuesday, a pancake race is run by women of 18 years and over. This race was first run, they say, in 1445 (another bit of history), and as you can imagine, the stories of how it got started are truly a fascinating read.

Even though getting to know the residents was a joy, looking after them on my own at night was a big responsibility. Sometimes if I sat too long in a chair between the rounds of checking on them and jobs that had to be done, I was always afraid of falling asleep, and when, during the night, a complete bed change was needed, and of course the care of the person, having to do this on my own was not always easy. Each morning, tea and breakfast for about nine persons then would have to be made and taken to each one of them while still in bed. Once they had finished, I would have to wash the breakfast things, leaving the kitchen tidy before the day staff arrived; but I think the hardest thing of all was having to get used to sleeping during the day, but I was never given the time to get used to doing this. It was not long before both he and the children became unhappy about me not being home during the night, and I was being urged to give the job up, but I had come to enjoy working there and spending time with the residents, so I decided, before giving in my notice to leave, I would ask my employer if there was any chance of changing my hours.

I was most surprised by his reaction, as he said that he was well satisfied with my work and so did not want me to leave. He said that he would sort something out as soon as possible and, by keeping his word; it was not long after that I began working the day shift.

Now everyone at home was happy 'it wasn't the job,' they said, it was just me working nights they did not like. Knowing that, I began to look forward to going to work each day; and because I spent more waking hours with the residents, some would tell me all about their life histories, which was sometimes sad, and some times funny. I remember how many of them had family photos leaning on the locker beside there bed; how they would tell me about their family as if the photo had been taken only yesterday, and when I saw how pretty or handsome some of the residents had been before age and sickness had taken over their lives, it told me how cruel old age could be.

I think it was about two years that I worked there. It's so hard to remember now, but then I began to feel that I needed a change; I felt I wanted to do something different, and even though I knew that saying goodbye to people I had grown fond of was going to be a sad day, I knew the time was right for me to leave. The question now was 'what can I do that is different,' and because he was working at this time, there was no pressure to take just any job that come along.

It was on a trip to Wolverton that I noticed in a shop window that they were looking for a sales person, and as I stood reading the advert I was asking myself 'would I like to do this sort of work again?' I remembered that I had worked in a shop many years before, so I was used to serving people, and because there were no fish involved, I say to myself 'at least I won't go home smelling of fish this time.' I had often passed the shop, which was like an Aladdin's cave, never dreaming that one day I would be asking to work there; and while I am thinking all this, I have opened the door and stepped inside.

I now find myself working once again in a shop, and even though I enjoyed working there, I do know I only stayed a short while. I had heard that a large store called "Marks & Spencer" was advertising for temporary staff to work over the Christmas period, and that sometimes temporary staff were made permanent afterward. This was a company that I really wanted to work for, as I had always been given the impression while growing up that working for Marks & Spencer was special. Why this was I do not know, but somehow this thought must have stuck with me, for, having heard that there were vacancies, I did not hesitate to apply to work for them, hopping that there may be a chance that I could have a permanent position once the holiday was over, and the surprise was that I did like working in a shop.

Marks & Spencer a large, worldwide retail company, which all started from a market stall back in the 1800's in an English northern town called Leeds, and this company which I found myself working for. Even though it was a job which kept you busy all the time, it was one I wish even now that I'd never had to give up, and as you reach this point in the sentence, I can here you asking 'if you liked the job that much, why did you leave; why did you give it up?'

It was a Sunday evening and we had been invited for an evening meal with friends. In the car was my youngest son, him and me. I remember slowing down to let a car cross in front of me from a petrol station, and it was only a few yards further on that from nowhere, I saw car lights heading straight for us. I remember trying to avoid them, knowing that they belonged to a vehicle that should not be where it was. I quickly turned the steering wheel, at the same time shouting out 'it's going to hit us!" But turning the steering wheel was to no avail, as the next second we met the car head on. It was my side of the car that took the most impact, but it ended up that he was the one who was hurt the most. Even though my knee and collarbone were injured, and my son, thankfully had only minor injuries, it was the hidden damage that was done to him that took me in a different direction on the road I am travelling.

Weeks went by and even though my son and I had recovered from the accident, he is still feeling unwell and continuing to say that there is something wrong with his neck, and he did not seem to have any grip in his right hand. On several occasions he had tried to go back to work, but was unable to grip the tools, and so was having to spend more time at home. At first it was suggested that maybe he had whiplash, but eventually he was sent back to the hospital; after further treatment, he was told that two of his vertebrae had lodged into his spinal cord. It was suggested that an operation could put this right, but because of the risk he decided that he did not want to take the chance. I said that I would go along with whatever he chose to do; after all it was he who would have to live with the outcome.

How was all of this now going to affect him? I wondered. He was unable to do the job that he had been trained for, and even though he had tried many other different jobs over the years plumbing was what he had always returned too.

At first he was very positive; he would continually go to the job centre or scan the local paper for a vacancy that he might be suited for, but after a while, when each time he went for an interview and had to tell them about his medical condition, he was never accepted.

Soon weeks turn into months, and the hope of him finding work fades, but he still tries, even taking a computer course. "Maybe I could get work in an office," he says, but his age and lack of experience, besides his disability, are all against him, till eventually he accepts that he will never work again.

All this time I have tried to keep his spirits up, but there are days when he complains of headaches and coldness in his hand, and as I write, I can hear him saying to me as he holds out his hand 'is my hand cold to you?' This is a question he would ask continually over the next few years, and sometimes, even though it was warm to me, I would say yes, knowing this would make him feel better.

For awhile I continued working for Marks & Spencer, but eventually I gave the job up as he was now receiving a benefit payment from the government; as I was only allowed to earn a certain amount of money, knowing that if I went over this, it would then be deducted from his benefit, it was not worth continuing to work.

How did I feel about leaving my job? The word I can honestly use was *unhappy*. After the accident they had been so supportive, and I had really enjoyed the time I had spent working for this company. I remember when I gave them my notice they had said they were sorry for me to go, and if ever I wanted to return, there would be a place for me, but of course that was never to be.

Once again time has moved on, and I have grandchildren who have brought a different type of joy into my life. Watching them grow reminds me of days long ago. I can hear all the phrases that I used to say, being said to them now by my children, and I know that they are thinking 'I never thought I would say that; I sound just like my Mum,' just as I had done and remembering has brought a smile to my face. As I write, I can hear the things she said to me once again, but this time there's no going off to make a cup of tea, just remembering the joy of my childhood makes me realise how lucky I am to have the memories I do.

How the car accident was to change our lives I would never have guessed at the time. No longer did we spend time away from home and each other. Now each day that passes has to be filled with finding things to do. We began spending more time in the garden, and going for walks along the canal; visiting other town centres when we could afford to put extra petrol in the car, and occasionally visiting my aunt in Greenford. But most of the time we spend at home. Then out of the blue, my second youngest son decided that it was time for him to leave home; it was not long after telling us this that he moved out and into new accommodation.

Time is moving on, and my youngest son has left school and because he is now working and has money of his own, has decided to buy himself a computer. As I have written that last word it reminds me of how times have changed, how technology has begun to take over our lives, for when I left school and started earning my own money, the nearest technology I came too was a record player that was now playing 45rpm records! But still, I must not grumble, as typing this record of my life on a computer is so much easier than having to have typed it on an old typewriter, and at least most of my bad spelling is corrected for me!

Next it was decided that the smallest bedroom upstairs was to be made into a computer room, where shelves would be fixed to the wall, and a desk built. As I listened to the conversation between him and my son, I think to myself 'I know where both of you are going to be spending much of your time in the future,' and I was right. Once the room was finished and my son was not using the computer, he would disappear, and sometimes, if he was not reading, I knew he would be tapping away on the computer keyboard. Now as I remember, I am asking myself: how did I feel about those days? Was I just as content as he had grown to be? I enjoyed the time that we could now spend with each other, but filling the days with the things we did had now become routine. As time rolled by, nothing changed, that is until I realised that he had begun to leave food on his plate - something which he had very rarely done, and when calling him when he was upstairs telling him his food was on the table, he would take ages coming down. He would then say the food was now cold, and did not feel like eating it; or complain I had put far too much on his plate, and he could not eat it all. It never occurred to me that anything was wrong with him, until I suddenly began to notice that he was loosing weight. I remember when I pointed this out to him and said 'you have got to eat more,' he just shrugged his shoulders and went upstairs.

It was just a few months later that we found out that he had cancer, and after a short stay in hospital, we were told that there was nothing that they could do for him. Over those months he had eaten less and less, which meant that his weight was falling at an alarming rate - so much so that even walking became difficult - until it was finally suggested that he should have a stay in the local Hospice. When this was suggested, it brought back memories of the time that my Mum too had stayed there, and I felt sick inside, but once there, he was helped to feel more comfortable.

I remember that time so clearly, of being taken into an office where the doctor tried to explain what I would have to face in the days ahead, but not really being able to take it all in, and not really believing all this was happening. All I seemed to hear were the words 'six weeks.'

Now all I could think of was 'what will I do without him,' but not even in my imagination could I comprehend the future, for all that had to be put on hold; now all I must think of is him.

Of course over those next weeks there were days when we were able to laugh, and times when I cried alone, until the last two weeks before he died, when I decided to spend not only the days with him but the nights as well, until he fell into a deep sleep and then passed away on the 8th of December, 2001, at the age of 64. (Time to make another cup of tea).

During this time, it was not only difficult for me, but of course the children as well. I remember how they would try to be cheerful, not letting on what was really going on inside of them, but I knew that they were only trying to keep cheerful for the sake of him and for me; of course, they could not believe what was happening, either.

Even now, when I look back and remember those dark days, I wonder, just like millions before me, how I survived, and I know now why I used the word 'survive' in the beginning when I opened up my memories.

I remember days of emptiness, hardly believing that he was no longer with me and of trying to fill a hole inside of me that was so big, nothing I did could fill it. Days passing and not realising that time was being filled with things I could not remember doing. If only I could bring him back, this ache inside of me would go, I kept saying to myself. But there was no bringing him back, and as the days turned into weeks, I still could not believe that he was not with me.

I remember listening for his footsteps on the stairs, expecting him any time to come down, and I could almost hear his voice asking me 'are you OK?' I felt sure I could hear him tapping away on the computer, and felt sure if I called out and told him his dinner was on the table he would answer 'I'll be there in a minute.' Would this feeling of hopelessness ever go away?

Several weeks had gone by when I felt it was time to empty my wardrobe of his clothes, for each time I opened the door, there they were staring at me; but as each item of clothing was laid on the bed, laying there beside it was the memory of him wearing it. I decided that I would keep one piece of clothing that I would put at the back of the wardrobe, knowing it would be there if I ever felt I had to just touch some thing that had been close to him.

Filling my days, as I remember, was the hardest thing of all. I felt sure that even though I had always been told there were 24 hours in a day, I now felt that this was not true, for there was no beginning to my day and no end, just time.

The one thing I was grateful for was the children, for even within there own grief, there was a place for me, as they gave of themselves unselfishly, spending as much of their time with me as they could, and that has continued to this day. I was also grateful that the City shopping centre was there, for I would spend each day walking round and round, just for something to do, hoping that while looking in the shop windows I would see, not him, but all that they had to offer.

As weeks turned into months I began to spend time with the friends that I had made during those dark days; friends who were in the same position as I was, and because they too are widows, understand whenever there is a day when I feel I cannot cope. Then one day I was asked by one of them if I would like to go to Paris for the weekend. 'Paris? I said, 'me go to Paris?' I had never been abroad and, never felt that I would ever step out of England, and here I was being asked to go on a train that would travel under the English Channel, to a place where I had only ever been in my dreams while sitting in a cinema. Paris: where even the name conjures up a fairy tale of imagination.

You will have to have a passport my friend said; again something I had never dreamt of owning. I did not even know how to go about getting one, but I need not have worried, for soon there I was, standing at a counter with a passport in my hand.

That weekend in Paris, standing looking out of a window at the Eiffel Tower, looking just like fairyland, as the lights that glowed in the dark brought a magic all it's own, had now opened up to me a whole new world of adventure, one I had never believed I could be part of, and a taste for travelling that I never knew I had, for it has not only been Paris but many parts of France since then that I have travelled to. I did not stop there; soon I was travelling to New York, visiting Times Square, Ellis Island and the Statue of Liberty; then on to Memphis, Tennessee, visiting Graceland (the home of the late Elvis Presley, whose music I had danced to as a young girl, the young girl who had never dreamt that one day would visit the place that he had lived and heard so much about). From there we travelled to White Rock, British Columbia, Canada, where, by the way does sit a large white boulder which, has a fascinating legend telling how it got there. We visited the wonderful city of Vancouver. But not only have I visited these countries and always enjoyed their hospitality; I have visited many parts of my own homeland, and have realised that the song was right, for I do live in a green and pleasant land.

So the road I was travelling on now had brought new adventures, and when I looked in the mirror, as I had done all those years ago as a young girl, looking back at me once again was a different person, one who had matured and survived despite all the twists and turns. Now I was travelling on roads that were taking me to places that I never dreamt of, and yet, even now, if any one had told me that there was still something inside of me that I had not yet discovered, I would never have believed them. So I was not prepared for the next adventure; one that has taken me three years to complete.

It all started one morning while standing in the kitchen with my grandson and my daughter. We had been talking about my Mum and Dad, and there I was talking merrily away, when all of a sudden my grandson said to me "Nan I wasn't there, I never knew them." It was only then that I realised that I had been speaking about them as if he had always been there; as if he had been part of their lives too, and then I realised that I was the only one who could tell the history as I knew and remembered it, about his Great Grandparents, my childhood, and my life with his Grand Dad.

I remember thinking 'we all want to know about our history.' There is something inside each of us that yearns to know how our families started. Something that makes us curious about the past, and so it was that I decided to write it all down, so that one day my children, grand children, and maybe their children, will read this and learn of their history, and know something of how their family began.

But how was I to begin? I had no idea, where would I start? What words would I use? Then I thought 'what a silly idea;' it takes me all my time to write a letter, let alone my memoirs. But I could not stop thinking about it, and even when I lay in bed, the thoughts would not go away. I knew that it was something I wanted to do, and because now my youngest son had also left home, the room upstairs where the computer had been, almost untouched over the years, began to draw me to it.

'First I must make this room mine,' I say to myself as I stand in the doorway and look around, remembering the times he had sat in the chair that now looked so cold and empty. I'll move the bookcase from one wall to the other; then I'll get rid of things that I no longer need. But my first job will have to be moving his plumbing tools, which are still under the desk; and so I started, but as I began to move the tools I saw, tucked away in his tool box, a small tin - Ill open that later I say to myself, as I carry on clearing out everything that is not needed.

Soon the room had taken on a new look, and then I remember the tin, and as I open it, staring at me are letters, and as I look closer, I see written on them S W A L K, and 'I love you', written in kisses. For a moment my heart skips a beat and then I realise that they were the letters that I had written to him so many years before.

I could not believe that he had kept them and hidden them away. How many times, I wondered, had he sat here in this room and taken them out to read them, or had thought about our years together, and all that we had been through, never saying a word, but could I open them now? How would reading them affect me? I had come a long way, and my grief was slowly healing, but I could not hold myself back, for soon I began to read the words that I had written all those years ago, and as I read my heart was back there. "To the one and only boy I shall ever love." "I love you," was on the first one I read, "I am looking forward to your coming home this weekend" were words on another. "I wish you could be with me all the time, not just weekends," and as I sat reading those words, I too began to remember the time when, sitting upstairs on the 607 bus, he asked me to marry him. I remember waiting for him to come home each weekend on leave, of standing on a platform waving goodbye, then the years that we had spent together, of the joy on his face as each time he had held his newborn child in his arms, and of the ups and downs and highs and lows that life had sent our way, and yet we had survived those years, and came through them. Keeping the promises we had made to each other; and as I go on reading, I know that even though he is not here with me now, just as I loved him then, I love him now, and as I hold the letters in my hand, I know that he loved me too. As I close the tin with the letters safe inside, I put them away, knowing I will bring them out again on another day, but for now, there is a new road and a story to tell.

THE END

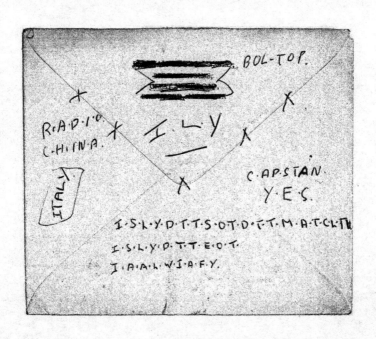

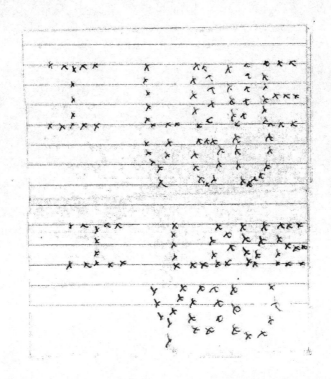

To the One & Only

Boy I shall always love,

My Dearest ■,

Just a line hoping your safe & well, This week is going nice & quick for me, is it for you. I hope so. Im looking forward to you comming home this week, as I realy miss you, so (Roll on) AM.

Im staying in to night to watch Tele, as it's very good on Wednesday nights.

Are you still doing nothing down at the work shops, I bet your finding it boreing, not like me at work, I'v had piles to do. Still I would prefore it that way. I do hope the weeknd will soon be here as I want's you with me so much, because I love you with all my heart, I realy do forever & always. I. LOVE YOU, I LOVE YOU I LOVE YOU x x x x x x x x xx

196